chicago 2nd ed.

P9-BYR-449

eat.shop chicago
was researched, photographed and written
by anna h. blessing

about eat.shop

the first thing to know about the *eat.shop guides* is that they are the only guides dedicated to just eating and shopping. okay, we list some hotels, because we know that you need to sleep. and don't forget to whittle out some time for cultural activities—all of the businesses featured in the book are helmed by creative types who are highly influenced by the arts, the architecture, the music and the overall verve of the cities they live in—culture is good for you.

the *eat.shop guides* feature approximately 90 carefully picked businesses, all of them homegrown and distinctive. some are small and some are big. some are posh and some are street. some are spendy and some require nothing more than pocket change. some are old school and some are shiny and new. some are hip and some are under-the-radar. point being, we like to feature a mix of places that are unique. places where you can feel the passionate vision of the owner(s) from the moment you step through their door, eat their food, touch their wares.

enough explaining, here are a couple of things to remember when using this guide:

1 > explore from neighborhood to neighborhood. note that almost every neighborhood that's featured has dozens of great stores and restaurants other than our favorites that have been featured in this book.

2 > make sure to double check the hours of the business before you visit. often the businesses change their hours seasonally.

3 > the pictures and descriptions of each business are representational. please don't be distraught when the business no longer carries or is not serving something you saw or read about in the guide.

4 > to truly experience the city chicago-style, hop on the el (www.yourcta.com). each businesses spread notes either the el stops of bus stops.

5 > this is the second edition of *eat.shop chicago*. there are more than 60 businesses new to this edition. if you would like to see the businesses that were featured in previous editions, they are listed on a following page. also their addresses and phone numbers can be found on the *eat.shop* website. and remember, don't get rid of your previous editions, think of them as just part of the overall "volume" of *eat. shop chicago*.

remember—every business that has been featured in this book, past and present, is fantastic. if the business is no longer featured in the book, it's not because we no longer love it, but because there are so many incredible establishments that are deserving to be noted. so make sure to reference the "past edition" list also, as many of chicago's true gems are on it and are not to be missed.

anna's notes on chicago

lately i have been quite the proud chicagoan, feeling a bit boasty about this city of mine. with a bid for the 2016 olympics, the building of calatrava's sky-high spire, and superstar mayor daley greening everything he can get his hands on, it's hard not to feel a bit braggarty. second city? says who?

as it rises on the international scene, chicago does so ever aware of its roots. in the two years since i did the first eat.shop chicago, amazing local shops and eateries have been shooting up in every neighborhood, and i'm thrilled to share my new favorites with you. this collection of businesses is what i think make up the personality of this city, from a brick-oven pizzeria, an organic bakery and an authentic thai spot, to a dog boutique, a designer collective, and a century-old german apothecary. it's the unique style of these business owners and their neighborhood shops, cafes, and restaurants that continue to make chicago as much a neighborly town as a big, busy city.

here are some of my favorite non-eat.shop things about chicago:

1> **the lakefront**: every easily accessible, fun-to-use inch of it makes this midwest city feel coastal, and means a day at the beach comes with an incredible skyline view to boot.

2> **real downtown life:** college kids, empty-nesters, and millennium park-lovers give the loop twenty-four-hour energy. we city dwellers truly dwell in the city.

3> **best-in-country architecture:** chicago is yet again the place for leading design. where else can you find the work of gehry, rem, and helmut mingling with mies, wright and goldberg?

4> **green and clean parks:** the city's crown jewel, millennium park, isn't the only exquisitely kept space; you'll find beautiful parks in every neighborhood of chicago that are good for yoga, picnics, afternoon naps and even the occasional outdoor nuptials

5> **access to the world:** one of the busiest airports is getting better every day, with nonstop flights all across the globe, so these infamously brutal winters can be escaped with just a little puddle hopping from o'hare.

okay. eat. shop. enjoy.

anna h. blessing
anna@eatshopguides.com

the master list

edgewater
eat:
moody's pub
ras dashen

andersonville
eat:
pasticceria natalina
shop:
scout
foursided

northwest side
eat:
smoque
tre kronor
shop:
american science & surplus
the swedish shop

wrigleyville / lakeview
eat:
hai yen
intelligentsia
pastoral
southport grocery & cafe
shop:
i.d. chicago
revival
twosided

lincoln park
eat:
bricks
sultan's market
sweet mandy b's
shop:
endo exo

gold coast
eat:
merlo on maple
sarah's pastries and candies

old town
shop:
a new leaf studio and garden
josephine
greer
the house of glunz

streeterville
eat:
fox & obel

river north
eat:
mk
pie
shop:
p.o.s.h.
le magasin
kara mann
white chicago

loop
eat:
intelligentsia

south loop
eat:
bongo room
custom house

lincoln square
eat:
bouffe
shop:
merz apothecary

north center
eat:
chalkboard

uptown
eat:
hai yen
tac quick

bucktown
eat:
milk and honey bake shop
sultan's market
the map room
shop:
apartment number 9
gem
p.45
raizy
red dog house
robin richman
roslyn
soutache
stitch

roscoe village
eat:
hot doug's
victory's banner
volo

wicker park
eat:
bongo room
milk and honey café
coco rouge
shop:
asrai garden
eskell
habit
hejfina
grow
nina
penelope's
porte rouge
saint alfred
the boring store

west town / ukranian village
eat:
dodo
feed
green zebra
juicy wine company
the bleeding heart bakery
shop:
alcala's western wear
komoda
rotofugi
sprout home
willow

logan square
eat:
bonsoirée
fonda del mar
lula café
the brown sack
vella café
shop:
wolfbait and b-girls

west loop
eat:
avec
blackbird
de cero
intelligentsia
sushi wabi
shop:
koros
ouest
primitive

previous edition businesses

andersonville
eat:
jinju
tweet

wrigleyville / lakeview
eat:
la creperie
pingpong
shop:
i.d. chicago
jake

lincoln park
eat:
athenian room
bourgeois pig
shop:
guise
the left bank
up down tobacco

old town
shop:
up down tobacco

gold coast
eat:
cru cafe and wine bar
shop:
jake
ikram

beverly
shop:
the original rainbow cone

river north
eat:
frontera grill
naha
rockit bar & grill
tizi melloul
shop:
blake
epoch

river east
eat:
japonais

lincoln square/ ravenswood / west lakeview
eat:
angel food bakery
bistro campagne
shop:
lulu's
modlife

uptown
eat:
tweet

bucktown
eat:
hotchocolate
irazu
jane's
le bouchon
red hen bread
scylla
the goddess and grocer
shop:
larkspur
tangerine
the painted lady
the red balloon co.
t-shirt deli

wicker park / west town
eat:
flo
matchbox
the silver palm
shop:
blake
lille
rr#1 chicago
salvage one

logan square
eat:
fat willy's rib shack

west loop
eat:
follia

you can find the addresses and phone numbers for all of these businesses at: eatshopguides.com

if businesses that were featured in a previous edition are not on this list, it means they have closed.

neighborhood boundaries : map info

north

edgewater
foster to devon, ravenswood
to lake michigan

andersonville
winnemac to bryn mawr,
ravenswood to broadway

east

wrigleyville / lakeview
diversey to irving park,
ravenswood to lake michigan

lincoln park
north ave. to diversey,
ashland to lake michigan

gold coast
chicago to north ave.,
dearborn to michigan ave.

old town
division to lincoln, cleveland
to clark

streeterville
chicago river to east lake
shore drive/oak, michigan
ave. to lake michigan

river north
kinzie to chicago, chicago
river to michigan ave.

loop
roosevelt to chicago river,
chicago river to lake michigan

south loop
22nd st. to roosevelt, clark to
lake michigan

west

lincoln square
montrose to bryn mawr,
chicago river to ravenswood

north center
diversey to montrose,
chicago river to ravenswood

bucktown
above-grade bloomindale
line to fullerton, western to
chicago river

wicker park
division to above-grade
bloomingdale line, western
to ashland

ukranian village
division to chicago,
western to damen

logan square
intersection of wrightwood,
milwaukee, kedzie and logan

west loop
congress to lake, ashland to
chicago river

roscoe village
belmont to addison, western
to ravenswood

directions

the neighborhoods to the left are broken down into geo-
graphical areas of the city.

the boundaries shown are what border the neighborhood
from north to south, east to west.

to make exploring chicago easier, remember it is on a grid
system, with state and madison streets at zero.

madison divides the north - south addresses, with in-
creases of 800 for each mile. state street seperates the east
- west addresses.

remember this information and you'll never be lost.

maps

because we wanted to give you the most detailed maps
possible, our city maps are now available on line.

please go to:

http://maps.eatshopguides.com/chicago_ed2/

here you will find a map of the entire city, with indicators
showing where each business is.

bookmark this url into your pda, and you'll have the
mapping data right with you as you explore.

if you don't own a pda, but want a great street map of the
city, the *eat.shop* authors love the *streetwise* maps. they are
indispensable tools when you need a take-along map with
lots of detail.

where to lay your weary head

there are many great places to stay in chicago, but here are a couple of my picks:

the james
55 east ontario street
877.526.3755 / 877.526.3755
jameshotels.com
standard double: from $379.00
restaurant: david burke primehouse
bar: jbar
notes: ultra-chic right off of the magnificent mile

w chicago city center
172 west adams street
312.332.1200 / 877.897.7091
starwoodhotels.com/whotels
standard double: from $239.00
restaurant: ristorante we
bar: the living room bar
notes: a great loop location

sofitel chicago water tower
20 east chestnut street
312.324.4000
sofitel.com
standard double: from $250.00
restaurant: cafe des architectes
bar: le bar
notes: contemporary style in the city center

hotel indigo
1244 north dearborn parkway
312.787.4980 / 866.521.6950
goldcoastchicagohotel.com
standard double: from $319.00
restaurant: the golden bean
bar: phi lounge
notes: gold coast location

anna's twenty favorite things

01 > brisket sandwich at smoque

02 > pastrami sandwich at the brown sack

03 > cannoli at pasticceria natalina

04 > finocchiona at juicy wine co.

05 > saffron almond milk at coco rouge

06 > taglioline paglia e fieno at merlo on maple

07 > assorted salumi at custom house

08 > royaltines at sarah's pastries and candies

09 > bo cuon banh trang wraps at hai yen

10 > stuffed french toast at vella cafe

11 > vintage pendant necklaces at gem

12 > bloom baby rocker at grow

13 > silver nikes at saint alfred

14 > anne black ceramics at the sweden shop

15 > lucite table at revival

16 > erica davies dress at roslyn

17 > tonfisk tea set at willow

18 > jimmie martin scorpion chair at kara mann

19 > magic amulets at primitive

20 > paul & joe shoes at ouest

avec

wine bar

615 west randolph steet. between jefferson and desplaines. green / pink lines : lake
312.377.2022 www.avecrestaurant.com
kitchen mon - thu 3:30p - midnight fri - sat 3:30p - 1a sun 3:30 - 10p
bar mon - fri 3:30p - 2a sat - sun 3:30p - 3a sun 3:30p - midnight

opened in 2003. owners: donnie madia, paul kahan and eduard seitan
chef: koren grieveson
$$ - $$$: all major credit cards accepted
dinner. first come, first served

west loop > e01

several years ago i found myself in london for thanks-giving, at a dinner party where, for the most part, i was surrounded by strangers. but because of the long table, the free-flowing wine, and the rich food, we were all best of friends by the night's end. *avec* reminds me of that night. it's where a community of strangers stretches out at essentially one long table. with the mix of amazing food and wine and being in a place so full of energy, you can't help feeling bound to everyone. just don't let things get so cozy that you lose track of your truffled focaccia.

imbibe/devour:
02 vina izadi, blanco
04 dievole-pachino, 'fourplay no.1'
chorizo-stuffed medjool dates
housemade red wine sausage
focaccia with taleggio, truffle oil & cheese
wood-fired pizza with housemade baccala
prosciutto di parma with red grapefruit

blackbird

a glorious restaurant

619 west randolph street. between jefferson and desplaines. green line : lake
312.715.0708 www.blackbirdrestaurant.com
lunch mon - fri 11:30a - 2p dinner mon - thu 5:30p - 10:30p fri - sat 5:30p - 11:30p

opened in 1997. owners: donnie madia, paul kahan, eduard seitan and rick diarmit
chef de cuisine: mike sheerin
$$ - $$$: all major credit cards accepted
lunch. dinner. full bar. reservations recommended

west loop >  **e02**

the first time i experienced *blackbird*, it was at my sister's birthday, upstairs in the party space. the second time i experienced *blackbird*, it was at my own birthday, downstairs in the dining room. this year is the beloved restaurant's 10th birthday, so now i will go to celebrate *blackbird's* birthday. if you're too shy to revel in your own passing years, then raise a toast to this place, more glorious than ever, with its superb bill of fare and flawless reputation. my birthday wish? another ten years for *blackbird*.

imbibe / devour:
02 ici/la-bas 'les reveles' oregon pinot noir
henriot souverain brut, reims n.v.
pinenut gazpacho
capriole old kentucky tomme cheese salad
monkfish with parmesan & prosciutto
slow-roasted sunset farm baby lamb
persille de malzieu with caramelized onions
mole beignet with goat's milk caramel ice cream

bongo room

decadent morning meals

wp: 1470 north milwaukee ave. between honore and evergreen. blue line : damen
sl: 1152 south wabash ave. corner of roosevelt. red/green/orange lines : roosevelt
wp: 773.489.0690 / sl: 312.291.0100 www.bongoroom.com
wp: mon - fri 7:30a - 2:30p sat - sun 9a - 2:30p / sl: mon - fri 8a - 2p sat - sun 9a - 2p

opened in 1993. owners: john latino and derrick robles. chef: john latino
$ - $$: all major credit cards accepted
breakfast. lunch. brunch. first come, first served

wicker park / south loop > **e03**

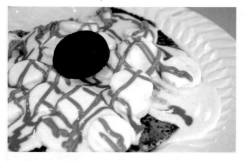

once upon a time, john and derrick had a place that was my top-favorite brunch spot around: *room 12* in the south loop. a tragic flooding shut the place down, and i was, to say the least, bummed out. until they reopened the spot, as bright as ever, as *bongo room* (number two). so don't despair if the line of people—waiting no doubt for those famous pancakes topped with oreos or ice cream—at the wicker park location is too long for your big appetite. just head to the south loop and get your sweet fix there, with a bit of peace and calm on the side.

imbibe / devour:
strawberry lemonade
bloody mary
oreo banana pancakes
lemon-buttermilk hotcakes
lump crab benedict
chicken & pear club sandwich
maple & mustard roasted pork loin sandwich
thai ginger chicken sausage

bonsoirée

café and underground restaurant

2728 west armitage avenue. at fairfield. blue line : california
773.486.7511 www.bon-soiree.com
dinner tue - fri 5 - 10p brunch sat - sun 9a - 3p underground restaurant on sat nite

opened in 2006. owner/chefs: kurt chenier and shin thompson
$$: all major credit cards accepted
dinner. brunch. byob. reservations recommended

logan square >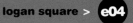

i'm not super good at keeping secrets, so i'm glad i wasn't the one to let this one out of the bag first. *bonsoirée* on saturday nights morphs into an "underground restaurant," whose limited-seating dinners are invite-only (you can sign up to be on their list). it feels a bit like a secret society, with your fellow pledgers surrounding you feasting on the chef's choice, five- or seven-course meal. for those who like to dine out in the open, and without ceremony, come any old day of the week when this off-the-beaten path gem is just as special as saturday.

imbibe / devour:
salad of asparagus & oyster mushrooms
wonton chips & edamame salsa
spicy red lentils, corn cake & fresh lime
toasted cumin gazpacho
pan roasted australian barramundi
grilled rack of lamb with baby fingerlings
bonsoirée's signature banana bread pudding

bouffe

gourmet food shop

2312 west leland avenue. between lincoln and western. brown line : western
773.784.2314 www.bouffechicago.com
tue - fri 11a - 7p sat 11a - 6p sun noon - 5p

opened in 2005. owner: tracy kellner
$ - $$: all major credit cards accepted
grocery

lincoln square >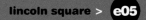

i have a confession. although a large part of my job involves shopping, i'll take a place like *bouffe* over an amazing shoe store or a spectacular product emporium almost any day of the week. it's not for my lack of love for shoes, *au contraire*. it's because of my near-addiction to gourmet and specialty food shops. i'm known to get giddy over never-before-seen mustards, or olive oils, or pasta sauces—the list goes on. so let it be known, *bouffe* is my version of shopper's heaven, and with libby reigning here, each season will be even better than the last.

imbibe / devour:
fizzy lizzy
french cheeses
bella cucina pasta sauces
french king's mustard
scappetti vodka pasta sauce
red hen bread
selection of olive oils
retro chocolate bars

19

bricks pizza

underground pizza

1909 north lincoln avenue. corner of wisconsin. brown / purple lines : sedgwick
312.255.0851 www.brickspetaluma.com
sun - wed 5 - 10p thu - sat 5 - 11p

opened in 1997. owner: bill brandt   chef: fernando mondragon
$ - $$: all major credit cards accepted
dinner. full bar. reservations recommended

lincoln park >

it's a risky thing in the city of pizza to stake claim on one pizza place and say that it's my favorite, what i think is the best pizza in town. but with *bricks*, i'm not risking so much, as i couldn't feel more confident in my pick. all you deep-dishers and stuffed-pizza fans may complain, as you won't find those styles here. but if you're craving crispy, cheesy thin-crust pizza loaded with toppings, head down into the dark cave-like den of *bricks* and dig into one of their pies. and don't forget to order a beer to offset the spice. it's imperative.

imbibe / devour:
fat tire beer
westmalle ales
caprese salad
baked goat cheese
ditka pizza
painful pizza
sweet heat pizza

chalkboard'

seasonal new american

4343 north lincoln avenue. corner of pensacola. brown line : western
773.477.7144 www.chalkboardrestaurant.com
mon, wed - sun 5 - 10p

opened in 2007. owners: gilbert langlois and elizabeth laidlaw chef: gilbert langlois
$$ - $$$: all major credit cards accepted
dinner. reservations recommended

north center > **e07**

i grew up spending summers in northern michigan, where there is a community that puts on musicals during the season: "kiss me kate," "guys and dolls" and other classics. when liz laidlaw starred in those plays, as she did on many occasions, no one could outshine her. well, she may have finally found her match, someone who might be able to steal the show with his stunning culinary creations—her husband, gilbert, chef of *chalkboard*. their toddler owen is on hand as well, but it's yet to be determined whether it's the stage or the stove that he'll rule.

imbibe / devour:
lillet blanc
chalkboard "75" cocktail
grilled brioche & blue cheese sandwich
smoked macaroni & cheese
free-range, hormone-free australian hanger steak
chalkboard salad
organic berries with lavender yogurt

coco rouge

luxe chocolate

1940 west division street. between wolcott and damen. blue line : damen
773.772.2626 www.cocorouge.com
tue - sat noon - 10p sun noon - 8p

opened in 2006. owners: erika panther and jeremy brutzkus
$ - $$: all major credit cards accepted
treats. online shopping. first come, first served

wicker park > 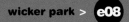 **e08**

i walked by *coco rouge* a dozen times before i finally entered, thinking, another chicago chocolate shop? come to find out, this is not another chocolate shop. this is *the* chocolate shop. caramelized leatherwood honey folded into bittersweet chocolate. velvety milk chocolate wrapped around raspberries infused with turkish rose oil. oh, my. erika and jeremy, creators of these exquisite truffles, also serve up opulent liquid chocolate, custom blends mixed with vanilla, pistachio or saffron. served hot or cold, these drinks will carry you through winter, right into summer.

imbibe / devour:
chocolate drinks:
  saffron almond millk
  madagascan single origin
truffles:
  leatherwood honey
  sirena
  miel a la lavande
  turkish coffee

custom house

a modern steakhouse

500 south dearborn street. corner of congress. red line : harrison
brown / orange / pink / purple lines : library-state / van buren
312.523.0200 www.customhouse.cc
breakfast mon - fri 7:30 - 10a sat 7:30 - 10:30a lunch mon - fri 11:30a - 2p
dinner mon - sat 5 - 10p sun 5 - 9p brunch sun 7:30 - 2p

opened in 2005. chef/owner: shawn mcclain
partners: sue kim-drohomyrecky and peter drohomyrecky
$$$: all major credit cards accepted
breakfast. lunch. dinner. brunch. full bar. reservations recommended

south loop > 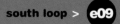 **e09**

chicago is considered by many a steak-and-potatoes town. and not without good reason—in some areas of the city, you'll find a classic, windy city steakhouse every few blocks, serving up fat porterhouses and mounds of steak fries. shawn mcclain has created a variation on this theme, so to speak, by taking a favorite dining custom and contemporizing it, to create *custom house*. from devout steak eaters to keen foodies, everyone is more than satisfied here, where the old school and the new school mingle at this instantaneously classic spot.

imbibe / devour:
garden cocktail
snake river fizz
assorted salumi
bone in short rib
swan creek farms rabbit
fingerlings with black truffle essence
buttermilk cake donuts
mint julep ice cream float

27

de cero

a modern taqueria

814 west randolph street. between halsted and green. green / pink lines : clinton
312.455.8114 www.decerotaqueria.com
lunch mon - fri 11:30a - 2p dinner mon - thu 5 - 10p fri - sat 5 - 11p

opened in 2004. www.decerotaqueria.com
$$: all major credit cards accepted
lunch. dinner. full bar. reservations recommended

west loop >

i've had many inquiries for restaurant recommendations in the past couple of years. from "where should I take my editor for a relaxed meal?" to "where should a group of friends celebrate a birthday that's fun but not crazy?" to "where is delicious mexican?" i hate to sound like a broken record, but *de cero* is my answer to all of these questions more often than not. across age, personality and style lines, *de cero* is always a pleaser. and after a couple of hibiscus margaritas, you will no doubt agree.

imbibe / devour:
hibiscus margarita
paloma
guacamole with housemade chips
chiles rellenos
al pastor taco
battered shrimp taco
ahi tuna taco
sorbet trio

dodo

home-cooked meals

935 north damen avenue. at walton. blue line : damen
773.772.3636 www.dodochicago.com
mon - fri 7a - 3p dinner 5 - 9p sat - sun 8a - 3p

opened in 2006. owners: kim dalton and william kasser chef: kim dalton
$ - $$: cash
breakfast. lunch. dinner. breakunch. byob. first come, first served

ukranian village > **e11**

as i ate at *dodo* with my sister, we marveled over the delicious corned beef hash, the tasty breakfast sandwich and the oh-so crispy bacon. after devouring everything, sarah delivered the best compliment she could give to a restaurant: the food felt home-cooked. meaning that kim has managed to produce that non-produced experience of a home-cooked breakfast—hearty, fresh and comforting. on a cold, chicago morning there's nowhere better than *dodo* to indulge in glorious, homey flavors. and the best bit? there are no dishes at the end of the meal.

imbibe / devour:
dodo daily hash bowl
tiramisu pancake
breakfast ciabatta sandwich
french toast
maple bananas
dodo special omelette
tofu scramble

31

feed

southern soul food
2803 west chicago avenue. corner of california avenue
773.489.4600
mon - sat 11a - 10p

opened in 2006. owners: donna knezek and liz sharp
$: cash
lunch. dinner. brunch. first come, first served

west town >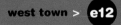

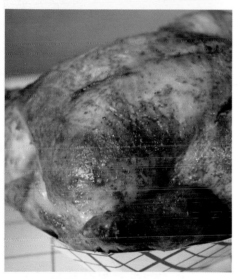

one of my sisters has a problem with meat on the bone. tragically, she'd have to miss out on the highly satisfying act of pulling almost-too-hot-to-touch chicken meat off of a whole bird at *feed*. this is a pure way of eating, getting to the meaty bits with your fingers, skipping the fork because it interferes with devouring. if you don't have the appetite for a whole bird, have a half; but no matter what, you've got to have the chicken here. and question to my sis: you can walk for miles in four-inch heels but can't pull meat off a bone? oh my...

imbibe / devour:
iced tea
lemonade
whole chicken
fried green tomatoes
handcut fries
fried catfish
mac-n-cheese
banana pudding

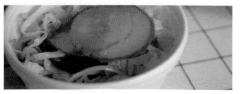

fonda del mar

mexican seafood

3749 west fullerton ave. between ridgeway and hamlin ave. blue line : logan square
773.489.3748 www.fondaonfullerton.com
dinner mon - thu 5 - 10p fri - sat 5 - 11p sun 4 - 9p
brunch sat 11:30a - 2p sun 11:30a - 3p

opened in 2005. owners: luis montero, raul arreola and angel hernandez
chef: raul arreola
$$: mc. visa
dinner. brunch. full bar. reservations recommended

logan square > 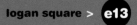 e13

there was a week earlier this summer when the weather was glorious: warm, sunny and not a drop of humidity. this weather draws chicagoans to the bustling waterfront, the river, and the outside patio at *fonda del mar*. no one would ever guess that a lush escape was tucked in the back of this restaurant, which sits on busy fullerton avenue. even on those not so dreamy days, when it's muggy and hot, this is still the place to come—a refreshing margarita and a plate of cochinita pibil is the ultimate escape.

imbibe / devour:
margarita rustica
bohemia beer
guacamole
ensalada fonda
mole manchamanteles
tilapia en salsa tropical
pozole de camarón

35

fox & obel

premier market and café

401 east illinois street. corner of mcclurg. red line : grand
312.410.7301 www.fox-obel.com
daily 7a - 9p

opened in 2001
$ - $$: all major credit cards accepted
breakfast. lunch. dinner. first come, first served
classes. free parking with purchase

streeterville > **e14**

i'm addicted to competitive chef shows, namely "top chef" and "iron chef." i love when the contestants are presented with an array of gorgeous ingredients to use for their challenge. when i'm at *fox & obel*, i feel like i'm in that world—without the time clock or tv cameras, of course. instead of racing around like a competitor on a reality show, i get to do the opposite and spend loads of time browsing every section looking for new arrivals. the only challenge here is being hungry at dinnertime, and thanks to the café in back, this is never a terribly hard problem to solve.

imbibe / devour:
house blend coffee
fresh baguettes
india tree baking sugar
vosges exotic truffles
everything from the butcher
red velvet cupcakes
bella cucina arrabiata pasta sauce
beautiful organic produce

green zebra

contemporary vegetarian

1460 west chicago avenue. corner of greenview. blue line: chicago
312.243.7100 www.greenzebrachicago.com
dinner mon - thu 5:30 - 10p fri - sat 5 - 11p sun 5 - 9p brunch sun 10:30a - 2p

opened in 2004. chef/owner: shawn mcclain
partners: sue kim-drohomyrecky and peter drohomyrecky
$$: all major credit cards accepted
brunch. dinner. full bar. reservations recommended

west town > **e15**

i love that shawn mcclain can totally master the meat scene at *custom house*—from roasted sweetbreads to grilled angus skirt steak and braised veal cheeks—and then, with a one-hundred-and-eighty-degree swing at *green zebra*, ditch the whole meat category to focus on eye-catching, immensely flavorful, seasonal vegetables. in a time when it's better than ever to be eating lower on the food chain, *green zebra* proves there's no sacrifice to be made by eating green. it's hard to find a carnivorous meal that is as jaw-droppingly gorgeous as the food here.

imbibe / devour:
rhubarb ginger ale
el tropicale cocktail
roasted beet panna cotta
roasted shiitake mushrooms in crispy potato
stinging nettles agnolotti
crisp chickpea pancake
apple butter beignets
black truffle chocolate chiffon

hai yen

vietnamese cuisine infused with french and chinese influences

ut: 1055 west argyle st. between kenmore and winthrop. red line : argyle
lp: 2723 north clark st. between diversey and wrightwood. brown / purple lines : diversey
ut: 773.561.4077 / lp: 773.868.4888 www.haiyenrestaurant.com
see hours on website

opened in 2000. chef/owner: hien ngo
$ - $$: all major credit cards accepted
lunch. dinner. first come, first served

uptown / lincoln park > **e16**

any experience i have had eating vietnamese food has involved loads of food. so my choice to accompany me to *hai yen* was my friend dave, known for his inhuman capacity to eat. we went straight for the five courses of meat and watched as our table piled high. as a testament to how incredible the food is here (and how skilled dave is), we finished off all five courses, two appetizers, a curry chicken, two vietnamese coffees, and a tapioca fruit shake. though not for the slight of stomach, this approach is highly recommended when eating the delicious fare at *hai yen*.

imbibe / devour:
green tea mango bubble tea
vietnamese coffee
vietnamese spring rolls
bo cuon banh trang wraps
pho ga soup
chao tom
papaya & mango salad
japanese eggplant stir-fried with tofu

41

hot doug's

the sausage superstore and encased meats emporium

3324 north california avenue. corner of roscoe street. cta bus : 152 - addison
773.279.9550 www.hotdougs.com
mon - sat 10:30a - 4p

opened in 2001. chef / owner: doug sohn
$: cash
late breakfast. lunch. early dinner. first come, first served

 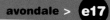

when i think hot dog, i think: bun, wiener, mustard. when doug thinks hot dog, he thinks something like: lamb. wild game. spicy smoked alligator. mango mayonnaise. belletoile cheese. roasted garlic. based off this list, it's no surprise that doug was the first in chicago to be hit with the illegal-foie-gras fee. you have to love a man who puts such passion into such a classic, once considered ho-hum item as the hot dog. yet with all his tinkerings with the dog, he doesn't forget its humble beginnings: as the chicago-style hot dog still takes top-of-the-menu real estate.

imbibe / devour:
green river soda
fanta
hot dogs:
  chicago-style
  the salma hayek: mighty, mighty hot
  the elvis: smoked & savory, just like the king
  spicy chipotle chicken sausage
duck-fat fries (friday & saturday only)

intelligentsia

coffee house

55 east randolph st. between michigan and wabash. brn/grn/pnk/org/prpl line : wabash
3123 north broadway st. between barry and briar. brown / purple lines : wellington
(see website for jackson location & hours for all stores) 312.920.9332 / 773.348.8058
www.intelligentsiacoffee.com

opened in 1995. owner: doug zell
$ - $$: all major credit cards accepted
coffee. light meals. treats. first come, first served

loop / lakeview / south loop > e18

i love a collaboration. shakira and wyclef. stella and adidas. madonna and britney. so i get excited every time i see *intelligentsia* at local eateries, especially when there is a collaborative blend: the *milk and honey* blend. the *avec* blend. the *blackbird* blend. the *lula café* blend. i've run out of fingers counting my favorite spots that brew this coffee. and yet, i do love to go straight to the source and grab a cuppa at one of their three locations or brew one of their amazing *intelligentsia* blends at home—might there be an *eat.shop chicago* blend in the picture?

imbibe / devour:
coffees:
  black cat espresso blend
  berkeley's blend
  flor azul from nicaragua
fox & obel muffins, scones & croissants
sugar and spice cookies & brownies
southport grocery granola bars & cupcakes
jerry's deli panini

juicy wine co.

bottle shop, cheese bar and lounge

694 north milwaukee avenue. between huron and erie. blue line: chicago
312.492.6620 www.juicywine.com
mon - fri 11 - 2a sat 11a - 3a sun 11 - 2a

opened in 2006. owner: rodney alex
$$: all major credit cards accepted
wine. light meals. first come, first served

west town > **e19**

my husband wants to buy a meat slicer. he talks about it almost every single time he opens a bottle of wine and inhales that perfect-with-meat, grape-pepper-cork scent. it's not that cured meats are something new to us, but the first visit to *juicy wine co.* and its "gotta-have-it-all" salumi selection turned a liking into an obsession. we're still a little tight on room for the industrial-sized slicer, but shawn, i promise i will make room someday. for now, *juicy* is the perfect place to get a fix for the addiction.

imbibe / devour:
adriano di suolo brunello di montalcino
two hands 'gnarly dudes' shiraz
dashe, zinfandel, dry creek valley
finocchiona
lamb prosciutto
queso y carne plate
esoteric spanish cheese plate
parmigiano-reggiano vacche rosse

lula café

farm-fresh food

2537 north kedzie boulevard. between linden and albany. blue line : logan square
773.489.9554 www.lulacafe.com
mon 9a - 10p wed - thu 9a - 10p fri - sat 9a - 11p sun 9a - 10p

opened in 1998. chef / owners: jason hammel and amalea tshilds
$$: all major credit cards accepted
breakfast. lunch. dinner. brunch. full bar. first come, first served

logan square > 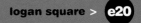 e20

for the past two years, when people ask me to name the place they must go if they go nowhere else in chicago, my reply is this: *lula café*. be it family visiting from out of town, strangers i meet halfway around the globe, locals looking for someplace they haven't tried, or chefs from other cities, my answer is the same. i have a distant love affair with *lula* as it's not in my neighborhood, sadly. i tell myself i would lose my passion if i went there too frequently, but word from logan square-ers is that it never tires: breakfast, lunch or dinner; daily, weekly or monthly.

imbibe / devour:
sambal bloody mary
lula sangria
mascarpone-stuffed brioche french toast
eggs florentine
moroccan chickpea sweet potato tagine
spicy peanut-butter tincka sandwich
olive oil marinated beet bruschetta

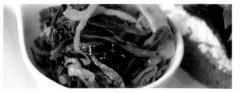

merlo on maple

an italian restaurant

16 west maple street. between state and dearborn. red line : fullerton
312.335.8200 www.merlochicago.com
daily 5:30p

opened in 2001. owners: giampaolo sassi and luisa silvia marani
chef: luisa silvia marani
$$ - $$$: all major credit cards accepted
dinner. brunch. full bar. reservations recommended

gold coast >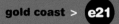

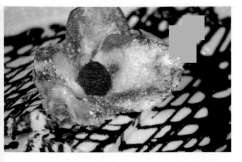

just off the hectic gold coast triangle sits this gem of a restaurant. silvia and giampaolo hail from bologna, and silvia, the chef, creates the miraculously delicate dishes from her homeland recipes. i love to come here and sit at the bar and dine, leaving not a bite of the house-made pasta on my plate. if you're torn—as i so frequently am—between the melt-in-your-mouth gnocchi, or the rich taglioline, or the pepper-crusted tuna, just ask bartender/server/authority-on-most-subjects david. he knows what you want even more than you do.

imbibe / devour:
03 vino nobile di montepulciano avignonesi
david's choice of vino
bresaola
tortelloni al burro e salvia
taglioline paglia e fieno
la rosa di parma
semifreddo di zabaione con cioccolato caldo

milk & honey

café and bake shop

café: 1920 west division street. between winchester and wolcott. blue line : division
bake shop: 1543 north damen ave. between north and pierce. blue line : damen
c: 773.395.9434 / bs: 773.227.1167 www.milkandhoneycafe.com
mon - fri 7a - 4p sat 8a - 5p sun 8a - 4p

opened in 2002. chef / owner: carol watson
$ - $$: all major credit cards accepted
breakfast. lunch. first come, first served

wicker park / bucktown >

are you an a.a. milne fan? i can't help but think of winnie the pooh with a pot of honey stuck to his nose when i see the jars of the same sweet stuff lining the back wall at *milk & honey café*. and i must admit, i feel a bit like pooh bear when i'm here because i want everything in sight: the sweet house-made granola, the lemon cookies, the raspberry rhubarb bread. the original location also has a stellar menu of sandwiches, but take note: the newer bake shop supplies only the sweet stuff. pooh would be so happy.

imbibe / devour:
bloody mary
raspberry vodka lemonade
lemon lavender cookies
house-made herb-crusted meatloaf
brussels sprouts with cracked mustard
milk & honey granola with yogurt
grilled chicken with bacon & lettuce sandwich
raspberry rhubarb bread

mirai sushi

japanese sushi restaurant

2020 west division street. between damen and hoyne. blue line : damen / division
773.862.8500 www.miraisushi.com
mon - wed 5 - 10p thu - sat 5 - 11p

opened in 1999. owner: miae lim chef: jun ichikawa
$$ - $$$: all major credit cards accepted
dinner. reservations recommended

wicker park >

there is a café in northern michigan i go to each summer. months go by, and i arrive wondering, will it be like it was? will it live up to my memory? but every time i walk in the door i realize how crazy my doubts were. *mirai* is like my summer café that never disappoints. it's been around for almost a decade and was first responsible for giving me serious raw-fish cravings. even after an extended absence, i can walk in and be reminded of how their fish has no peer. the rolls are tasty too, and they even have a few warm treats if you so desire. but first and foremost, this is the place for fish.

imbibe / devour:
hirame usuzukuri
bin cho
spicy tar-tar
gyoza ravioli
ungari trio
ebi togarashi
kani nigri

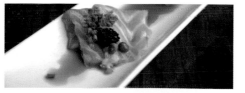

mk

a restaurant focusing on seasonal ingredients
868 north franklin st. between chestnut and locust. brown / purple lines : chicago
312.482.9179 www.mkchicago.com
sun - thu 5:30 - 10p fri - sat 5:30 - 11p

opened in 1998. chef/owner: michael kornick executive chef: erick simmons
$$ - $$$: all major credit cards accepted
dinner. full bar. reservations recommended

river north >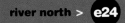

as we've gotten older, my family has grown, adding new family members to the mix with each marriage. on the night after my brother's wedding, my family, and our second halves, needed a place to celebrate. without a moment's hesitation, *mk* was our choice. we sat around the table, dipping our pommes frites into truffled cream, drinking wine, talking over each other, eating one another's food and licking our plates clean. the meal met our moods, from start to finish, leaving us all happy and in agreement—truly a feat for a big, unruly family like ours.

imbibe / devour:
the ipanema cocktail
north shore negroni
green garlic soup
charcoal grilled rack of lamb
peppercorn-crusted yellowfin tuna
pan-roasted pacific halibut
pommes frites with truffle cream
angel food cake

moody's pub

pub and beer garden

5910 north broadway street. at thorndale avenue. red line : thorndale
773.275.2696 www.moodyspub.com
mon - sat 11:30a - 1a sun noon - 1a

opened in 1959. owners: john and jake moody
$: cash
lunch. dinner. first come, first served

edgewater > **e25**

on a recent trip to germany, shawn and i found ourselves enjoying a sunny seat at a beer garden. big mugs of beer, savory bites, people-watching galore—i sat wishing there was such a place back home until i realized there was: *moody's pub*, an outdoor beer garden paradise in the summer, with what some bill as the best burger around. because chicago's climate pushes us indoors much of the year, revel in the garden here whenever you can. but when you can't, cozy up in the huge indoor tavern, where warming fires burn, the grill is replete, and beer flows freely.

imbibe / devour:
berghoff dark lager
summer crush cocktail
moodyburger
the moody bleu burger
fried seaburger
sloppy joe
onion rings
fresh-cut house fries

pasticceria natalina

an italian pastry shop

5406 north clark street. between balmoral and rascher. red line : bryn mawr
773.989.0622
wed - fri 9a - 7p sat 9a - 5p sun 11a - 5p

opened in 2007. owners: natalie and nick zarzour
$ - $$: mc. visa
treats. first come, first served

andersonville >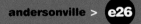

when natalie was touring me through the sicilian pastries she was offering for the day at *pasticceria natalina*, she ended finally with their number-one seller, cannoli, because, "everyone loves cannoli." i, however, have never loved cannoli. until i met nick and natalie. they painstakingly create the crispy shells each day and wait to fill them until they've been ordered, so that each one is fresh. these cannoli were so perfect, i did everything i could not to eat two in one sitting. needless to say, i'm a serious cannoli convert, that is, as long as they are from *pasticceria natalina*.

imbibe / devour:
espresso
barca di crema
baba al rum
sfogliatelle
crostata al limone ai frutti del bosco
dannoli
cassatine
pignolate

pastoral

artisan cheese, bread and wine

lv: 2945 north broadway st. between wellington and oakdale. brn / prpl lines : wellington
el: 53 east lake street. corner of wabash. brn/grn/org/pnk/prpl/red lines : state / lake
773.472.4781 www.pastoralartisan.com
tue - fri 11a - 8p sat 11a - 7p sun 11a - 6p

opened in 2004. owners: ken miller and greg o'neill
$$: all major credit cards accepted
grocery. first come, first served

lakeview / east loop > **e27**

before i learned to love real cheese (i.e. stinky cheese), i had a pretty basic cheese education. my grade school field trip to oregon's tillamook creamery kicked off the training, and i fell in love with the bright orange loafs of cheddar. years later, a french exchange student convinced me that brie on baguette was the ultimate sandwich. then a stint in italy had me fawning over parmigiano reggiano. my adult education, however, is centered at *pastoral*. here you'll learn that cheddar doesn't have to be orange, french cheese is more than brie, and the older and smellier, the better.

imbibe / devour:
pleasant ridge reserve
05 verdad rose, central coast, california
peny picot camembert
matiz piquillo peppers
manchego artisano
idiazabal sheep's milk cheese
chorizo espanol

63

pie

a pie shop

615 north state street. between ontario and grand. red line: grand
312.642.4192 www.piechicago.com
tue - sat 10a - 5p

opened in 2007
owners: mike hines, mikel laughlin, dara shlifka, aric shlifka and michael rivitto
$ - $$: all major credit cards accepted
treats. first come, first served

river north >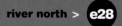

i think pie has gotten a bad rap for the past decade or so. first, it doesn't get much play as it's seasonal—pumpkin at thanksgiving, mincemeat at christmas, cherry for fourth of july. second, it's associated with a plump, grandmotherly baker dressed in a scallop-edged apron. take those visions and toss them, and meet chicago's *pie*, brought to us in part from the same duo who created *epoch floral design*. homey pies are baked fresh daily and sold from the updated, cool environs in the tree studios space. grandmothers and foodies alike are sure to be pleased at *ple*.

imbibe / devour:
pies:
  classic apple
  maple pecan
  lemon chess
  peanut butter
  key lime
  banana cream
  meringue

ras dashen

ethiopian restaurant

5846 north broadway street. between thorndale and hollywood. red line : thorndale
773.506.9601 ww.rasdashenchicago.com
daily noon - 11p

opened in 2001. chef / owner: zenash beyene
$: all major credit cards accepted
lunch. dinner. full bar. reservations recommended for six or more

edgewater > 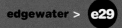 **e29**

i love a twist on the usual spoon, knife and fork combo of eating utensils. for example, the spork makes meals feel like a multi-tasking activity. chopsticks test dexterity, but i'm up for the challenge. at *ras dashen*, all eating tools are out the window. hallelujah, freedom from the tools. in traditional ethiopian style, you sop up everything with porous injera or dig into piles of lamb and chicken with your built-in tools: your fingers. and in the end, no spork, nor fork could be half as satisfying a utensil as your own bare hands.

imbibe / devour:
bedele beer
hakim beer
yeqaysur salata
kik alicha
doro alicha
yebeg wat
bread pudding

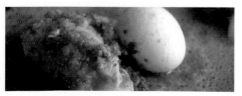

sarah's pastries and candies

delicious enticements

70 east oak street. between michigan and rush. red line : chicago
312.664.6223 www.sarahscandies.com
tue - thu 8a - 7p fri - sat 8a - 9p sun 10a - 6p

opened in 2005. owner: sarah levy
$: all major credit cards accepted
treats. first come, first served

gold coast > e30

sarah, liza, nora, holly and i shared a place together our senior year in college. if a mom forgot to call on a birthday, or there was a nasty break-up, or a wicked final exam and no sleep—we knew we would be okay because we had sarah's cakes. they cured all and were often filled with a surprise—like crispy caramel crème brûlée, and always coated in buttercream. since sarah is no longer my roommate, i'm relieved to live near her wonderful store, *sarah's pastries and candies*, where i can still get her decadent cakes and addictively crispy, crunchy chocolate delights and royaltines.

imbibe / devour:
coffee
macchiato
black & white cupcakes
blueberry muffin
specialty cakes
chocolate delights
royaltines

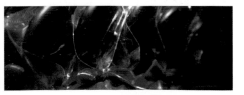

smoque

low and slow bbq

3800 north pulaski road. corner of grace street. blue line : irving park
773.545.7427 www.smoquebbq.com
tue - thu 11a - 9p fri - sat 11a - 10p sun 11a - 9p

opened in 2006. owners: barry sorkin, al sherman,
chris hendrickson, mike mcdermott and oscar romero. chef: robert brown
$ - $$: all major credit cards accepted.
lunch. dinner. first come, first served

northwest side > **e31**

the first time i tried *smoque*, i'd just come back from a trip to the south, where pulled pork and ribs had been my daily fare. i'd had my fill of slow-cooked pig. or so i thought, until i stepped into *smoque* and tucked in to a heaping pile of vinegary pulled pork and a side of hot, hand-cut fries. one note i jotted down while gorging was, "pay attention to the sides." this is imperative folks: don't get skip out on the sides or you'll miss the hot cornbread, fresh slaw, and oozing peach cobbler. i'll leave it to you to find the room in that belly of yours.

imbibe / devour:
sweet tea
baby back ribs
pulled pork sandwich
brisket
cornbread
fries
cole slaw
peach cobbler

southport grocery and cafe

exquisite, upscale grocery and cafe

3552 north southport avenue. between addison and cornelia. brown line : southport
773.665.0100 www.southportgrocery.com
mon - fri 8a - 7p sat 8a - 5p sun 8a - 3p

opened in 2003. chef / owner: lisa santos
$$: all major credit cards accepted
breakfast. lunch. first come, first served

lakeview >

here's a little tale. it's called the *southport grocery* cupcake craziness. once upon a time, *southport* made a simple white cupcake. as it turns out, it wasn't so simple after all, for it soon gained status as best in town, drawing in sweet-toothed patrons from every corner of the city and making the bakers at *southport* busy busy busy. the end. but here's my coda. though *southport* takes the cake for this goodie, i remind the readers of this tale to pay heed to the masterful menu of other delightful treats and glorious grocery picks at this kingdom of goodness.

imbibe / devour:
cappuccino
hot chocolate
the cupcake
hot dog
breakfast hash
salami, prosciutto & fig salad
home-roasted nuts
chocolate toffee scone

73

sultan's market

middle eastern deli

wp: 2057 west north avenue. between damen and hoyne. blue line : damen
lp: 2521 north clark street. between deming and st. james. red/brown/purple : fullerton
wp: 773.235.3072 / lp: 312.638.9151 www.chicagofalafel.com
mon - thu 10a - 10p fri - sat 10a - midnight sun 10a - 10p

opened in 1990. owners: the ramli family
$: all major credit cards accepted
lunch. dinner. first come, first served

wicker park / lincoln park > **e33**

my husband recently spent two weeks in the middle east. he regaled me daily with stories of fantastic feasts of kebabs, tabbouleh, stuffed grape leaves and more. i was having a pity party for myself that i was missing out on such culinary delights until i set foot into *sultan's market* and remembered that i had my own little piece of middle eastern cuisine right here, with a falafel sandwich that can't be matched anywhere. i was immediately cheered-up and stuffed full with falafel. i didn't have to miss out on all those delights after all—just the belly dancers.

imbibe / devour:
tamarind juice
spinach pie
zatter bread
lentil soup
rice & lentils
spicy falafel sandwich
chicken shawerma

sushi wabi

japanese restaurant and sushi bar

842 west randolph street. between green and peoria. green line : clinton
312.563.1224 www.sushiwabi.com
lunch mon - fri 11:30a - 2p dinner sun - tue 5 - 11p wed - sat 5p - midnight

opened in 1998
$$ - $$$: all major credit cards accepted
lunch. dinner. reservations recommended

west loop > **e34**

you've heard of writer's block, but you may not have heard of eater's block. yes, such a thing exists. it's when your taste buds feel sluggish, you feel no love for any flavors, and all food looks the same. this is the time to come to *sushi wabi*, the ultimate palate cleanser and eater's-block eradicator. the streamlined interior gives way to immaculate and gorgeous food. each roll is a beautiful artistic work with tastes that will jolt you out of your food hum-drum. ahhh, now if only i had such a quick cure for writer's block.

imbibe / devour:
pineapple hii cocktail
momotaro cocktail
hot grilled asparagus
maki:
   godzilla
   spider
   rainbow
grilled pineapple with fresh berries

77

sweet mandy b's

old-fashioned desserts

1208 west webster avenue. between racine and magnolia. brown line : armitage
773.244.1174
sun - thu 8a - 10p fri - sat 8a - 11p

opened in 2002. owner: cindy levine
$: all major credit cards accepted
treats. first come, first served

lincoln park >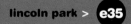

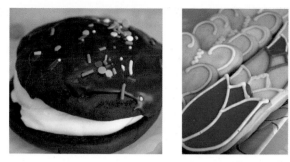

when i see the s'mores here, i think of my dad, who would love them, in their contained, pre-created safeness. bear with me. most might not label *sweet mandy b's* as a safe haven, but you have to understand the fearsome relationship my father has with marshmallow roasting. with the open flame, rambunctious kids, and "flaming sticks" (my dad's term), he sees s'more-making as an eye-poking catastrophe waiting to happen. so the dangerous s'mores at *mandy b's* would satisfy his craving—for safety. for the rest of us, the treats here are just dangerously good.

imbibe / devour:
red velvet cupcakes
peanut butter cookies
s'mores
chocolate gingerbread cookies
miniature cupcakes
chocolate cream pie
caramel apple cake

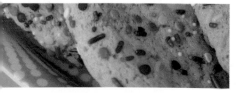

tac quick

authentic thai

3930 north sheridan road. corner of dakin. red line : sheridan
773.327.5253
mon 11a - 10p wed - sat 11a - 10p sun 11a - 9:30p

opened in 2003. chef / owner: andy aroonrasameruang
$ - $$: all major credit cards accepted
lunch. dinner. byob. first come, first served

lakeview >

if you think the regular menu at *tac*—short for thai authentic cuisine—is authentic, then the thai menu, which you have to request to receive, is doubly so. you can choose from the thai classics here like pad thai, which has no match, and flavorful satays, or you can take a few authentic adventures off of the thai menu, like the crispy, crackly fish maw, or the isaan sausage, or the grilled pork neck. i can assure you, the more you stick your own neck out, the happier you'll be at *tac quick*.'

imbibc / devour:
thai iced coffee
yum kra por plaa salad
chicken satay
spicy basil rolls
panang curry
som tum salad
phad phet plaa duk

the bleeding heart bakery

organic bakery and café

1955 west belmont avenue. between damen and wolcott. brown line: paulina
773.278.3638 www.thebleedingheartbakery.com
tue - sat 7a - 7p sun 8a - 6p

opened in 2007. chef/owners: michelle and valentin garcia
$ - $$: all major credit cards accepted
breakfast. lunch. brunch. first come, first served

north center > 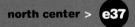 **e37**

there's a joke i once heard: if you're not a liberal in your youth, then you have no heart. if you're not a conservative in old age, then you have no brain. conservative or liberal, young or old, you're simply a downright dummy with neither heart nor brain if you're not head over heels for *the bleeding heart bakery*, a true independent. this place is the country's first usda-certified organic bakery, where the sustainable goods taste delish and are most-deserving of a little bleeding-heart love, from both donkeys and elephants alike.

imbibe / devour:
lavendar lemonade
take-a-hike scone
s'mores brownie
bleeding heart shorbread cookies
dutch letter cookies
ginger molasses
chicago symphony cake
black bean burger

the brown sack

soup, sandwich and shake shack

3706 west armitage avenue. corner of lawndale. blue line : logan square
773.661.0675
tue - sun 11a - 7p

opened in 2006. owner: malaika marion
$ - $$: all major credit cards accepted
lunch. dinner. first come, first served

logan square >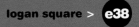

my parents are high school sweethearts. that they are celebrating their 40th anniversary soon is because of two things: my mom's spaghetti and my dad's pastrami sandwich. so good is his sammie, my mom, usually unexcitable, still goes on about it in raptures. i'm quite thankful that my new favorite sandwich and shake shop, *the brown sack*, wasn't around back when my parents were at lyons township high, for if my mom had tried malaika's version, she might have left my dad and his pastrami in the dust. dad, your 'wiches are good, but malaika, yours are glorious.

imbibe / devour.
chocolate shake
root beer float
vegan chili
corned beef reuben
extra cheesy macaroni & cheese
blt sandwich
homemade sloppy joe
almond bark drop cookies

the map room

a traveler's tavern

1949 north hoyne avenue. corner of armitage. blue line : western / milwaukee
773.252.7636 www.maproom.com
mon - fri 6:30a - 2a sat 7:30a - 3a sun 11a - 2a

opened in 1992. owner: mark blasingame
$ - $$: all major credit cards accepted
drinks. first come, first served

bucktown >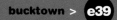

in my grandfather's home, there is a big map of the world, with round-head pins marking all of the places he has visited. my grandfather is 85 years old and a million-mile traveler, so there are a lot of pins. i wonder, if *the map room* used one of its big maps to put a pin everywhere their beer has come from, whose map would be more packed with pins. we'll never know, but one thing i do know is that this truly is a traveler's tavern, as they say. this is the bar to settle into when you're itchin' for a taste of another place and several hundred tastes of beer that is. happy travels.

imbibe / devour:
lindemans framboise lambic beer
north coast red seal ale
great lakes blackout stout
oakham asylum beer
koningshoeven trappist beer
brewster's mati hari beer
fantôme printemps belgian beer

tre kronor

a scandinavian restaurant

3258 west foster avenue. corner of sawyer. brown line : kedzie
773.267.9888 www.swedishbistro.com
mon - sat 7a - 10p sun 9a - 3p

opened in 1992. owners: patty rasmussen and larry anderson
$ - $$: all major credit cards accepted
breakfast. lunch. dinner. first come, first served

northwest side >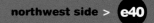

i shouldn't be the one writing about *tre kronor*. my friend katie, who first turned me on to this spot, should be. she describes it as a place where apple-cheeked girls come offering that day's selection of fresh pastries, only to be followed with a hearty heaping of pancakes, waffles, or housemade quiche. this is wholesome central, straight from the folks who own *the sweden shop* across the street. for a sunday smorgasbord, dig in at *tre kronor*. and don't miss the classic homemade cinnamon roll, i guarantee it'll make you feel like swedish royalty.

imbibe. / devour:
espresso
fresh-squeezed o.j.
danish-style pastries
classic swedish cinnamon roll
belgian waffle with fruit & whipped cream
pannekaker
quiche of the day
housemade pickled herring

vella cafe

panini shop and more

1912 north western avenue. corner of milwaukee. blue line : western
773.489.7777 www.vellacafe.com
mon - fri 7a - 3p sat - sun 9a - 3p

opened in 2007. owners: sara voden and melissa yen
$: all major credit cards accepted
breakfast. lunch. byob. first come, first served

logan square > **e41**

since i work from home, i don't have a commute. a prof of mine in grad school said once that when he free-lanced, he had to get dressed, walk around the block, and "go to work," or it was a robe and slippers for the day. i am not so diligent about forced commutes, but i might change my ways for the commuter specials at *vella*. a steaming hot sandwich, or stuffed french toast, might make me leave the house. sitting right below the el, *vella* couldn't be more perfectly placed for those lucky blue liners. just remember to change out of your robe and slippers before you come.

imbibe / devour:
cafe de olla latte
yerba maté
cinnamon apple crepes
stuffed french toast
butterkase & roasted tomato panino
peanut butter, chocolate & banana panino
smashers

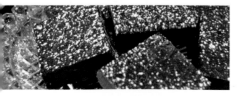

91

victory's banner

vegetarian food with indian flavors

2100 west roscoe street. corner of hoyne. brown line : addison
773.665.0227 www.victorysbanner.com
mon, wed - sun 8a - 3p

opened in 1999. owner: pradhan balter. chef: erin mullen
$ - $$: all major credit cards accepted
breakfast. lunch. first come, first served

roscoe village >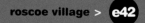

it's no wonder that *victory's banner* was first recommended to me by my yoga teacher. you're bound to find a touch of brightening enlightenment here, where inspiration and meditation is served up with a vegetarian fare of indian-influenced dishes. the french toast is without equal in its thick, golden goodness and capable of inspiring total loving goodwill toward world and self. sometimes nirvana is reached by just being; sometimes it's reached by just eating. namaste.

imbibe / devour:
mango lassi
raspberry iced tea
french toast
brahma burritos
the curry omelette
bliss burger
ultimate waffle
uppama

volo

restauarant and wine bar
2008 west roscoe street. between damen and seeley. brown line : addison
773.348.4600 www.volorestaurant.com
mon - thu 5p - midnight fri - sat 5p - 2a

opened in 2005. owners: jon young and stephen dunne chef: stephen dunne
$$: all major credit cards accepted
dinner. full bar. reservations recommended

roscoe village > 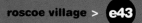

i love a wine flight. the trio keeps up with my over-zealous attitude of wanting to try a little bit of everything and promises that i won't be bored and am bound to find a favorite. *volo*, italian for flight, takes that idea and applies it to the whole restaurant, with a menu where you get to nibble and sample, and a space that lets you choose a cozy corner booth, a high stool at the bar, or a seat in the dreamy outdoor garden. *volo* is a chic enoteca, comfy neighborhood restaurant, and classic wine bar all in one, a dream come true for the flighty among us.

imbibe / devour:
04 warwick, pinotage, stellenbosch
spanish reds flight
steak tartare
sweet pea pizza
braised lamb shoulder pot pie
italian sausage stuffed cabbage rolls
grana padano
vintage gouda

eat

a new leaf studio and garden

floral shop and event space
1818-1820 north wells street. corner of lincoln. brown / purple lines : sedgwick
312.642.8553 www.anewleafchicago.com
mon - sat 9a - 7p sun 10a - 6p

opened in 1973. owner: marion parry
all major credit cards accepted
events

old town > 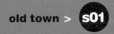 s01

i used to live around the corner from *a new leaf*, and i'd pass by its crowded bunches of tulips and lilies lining the sidewalk every evening on my walk home. last summer ago, my friends katie and john had their wedding reception at *a new leaf's* event space, where the party spilled out onto the secret garden-esque courtyard in the back for most of the night. i realized then that everything here is magical, from store to event space—neither ls to be missed. and remember, don't leave without a gathering of scented blooms.

covet:
all variety of cacti
green orchids
azaleas
large, potted plants
gorgeous bouquets
glassware & pots
a succulent garden
a party in the event space

alcala's western wear

cowboy boots, hats and gear

1733 west chicago avenue. between paulina and wood. blue line: division
312.226.0152 www.alcalas.com
mon 9:30a - 8p tue - wed 9:30a - 7p thu - fri 9:30a - 8p sat 9:30a - 7p sun 9:30a - 5p

opened in 1972. owners: richard and robert alcala
all major credit cards accepted
free parking. free tailoring while you wait. hat cleaning and shaping

west town >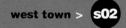

levi's jeans and cowboy boots have a special place in american culture, and whether you live in rural farmland or the big city, you've probably owned both at some point in your life. the best spot in this town to stock up on said getup is *alcala's western wear*, where thousands of boots line the wall, levi's are stacked high and the air smells like cowhide. there's nothing quite like *alcala's* in the city, which doesn't feel so much like the city as the country, and where you can find one-of-a-kind cowboy boots of every skin, color and pattern you could dream of.

covet:
dark straight-leg levi's
alligator cowboy boots
buckles
leather-tooled belts
turquoise & silver jewelry
minnetonka moccasin boots
stetson straw hats

american science & surplus

a catch-all for science, crafts, supplies and surplus

5316 north milwaukee avenue. at foster. cta bus: 85 / 68
773.763.0313 www.sciplus.com
mon - wed 10a - 7p thu 10a - 8p fri 10a - 7p sat 10a - 6p sun 11a - 5p

opened in 1937. owner: philip cable
mc. visa
online shopping

northwest side > 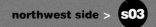 **s03**

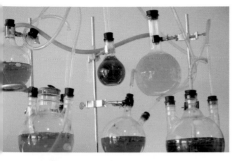

everyone has a favorite grade-school science teacher and mine was mr. vanderhyde: a lanky, bespectacled instructor who fit the role of mad scientist—or so it seemed to us fourth graders. mr. vanderhyde would have loved *american science and surplus*, which brings me back to grade school days of making baking soda explode with vinegar from a papier-mâché volcano, and pouring mysterious liquids from one beaker to another. here you can find all the equipment needed to be an amateur scientist, prankster, engineer, rock collector or general amasser-of-neat-things.

covet:
silly putty
original slinky
glass science beakers
agate slab
bestest maggots ever!
marbles
ph paper
pirate's creed of ethics

apartment number 9

a modern men's clothing store
1804 north damen avenue. between churchill and willow. blue line : damen
773.395.2999
mon - fri 11a - 7p sat 11a - 6p sun noon - 5p

opened in 2001. owners: sarah and amy blessing
all major credit cards accepted

bucktown >  s04

here's the blessing family story as it pertains to *apartment number 9*. middle sister, amy, talks up every human body who sets foot inside, doling out advice and opinions on any topic that comes up, including what to wear. oldest sister, sarah, fixes out-of-place collars, cinches ties, and helps men looking for such assistance. our mom creates, making super-soft, handknit hats with intricate cable stitches and laborious fair-isle patterns. and i, the youngest blessing sister, get the job of telling everyone i know about the most wonderful men's store around.

covet:
martin margiela boots
dries van noten hand-embroidered scarves
band of outsiders vintage fabric ties
seize sur vingt custom-made shirts
rogues gallery dead weights necklaces
paul smith suits

105

asrai garden

1935 west north avenue. between damen and wolcott. blue line: damen
773.782.0680 www.asraigarden.com
mon - sat 10a - 7p sun noon - 4p

opened in 1999. owner: elizabeth cronin
all major credit cards accepted
deliveries. weddings. events

wicker park > 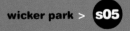 s05

i love flowers, flower shops, and all things floral, but so often flowers are either super-duper fussy and/or frilly. flowers are wild and exquisite and intricate, so why try to rein that in or fancy that up too much? elizabeth at her colootial *asrai garden* doesn't try to do either. she just creates ethereal and expressive works of art, putting together exotic blooms that are both sexy and a bit edgy. while you're picking up blooms for a friend, get a little something for yourself in the way of santa maria novella or one of the shop's lavish products.

covet:
palya organic body & face care
korres basil lemon body water
côté bastide everything
santa maria novella weekend soaps
eskander ginger blossom candle
claus porto soaps
flowers, flowers, flowers

107

endo exo

sleek beauty boutique

2034 north halsted street. between armitage and dickens. brown / purple lines : armitage
773.525.0500 www.endoexo.com
mon - fri 11a - 7p sat 10a - 6p sun 11a - 5p

opened in 1999. owner: stephanie salerno walls
all major credit cards accepted
classes

lincoln park > 

everyone needs a little makeover once in awhile, and it was here at *endo-exo* that i came for a makeup lesson and application, and to restock and refresh my cosmetic collection. i learned helpful techniques and loaded up on recommended products that have now become essentials. but more importantly, i got super pretty lip glosses, a perfect rosy blush and the best mascara in the world. don't you love when you can be a bit girly, yet practical and grown-up all at once? *endo exo* is just the place—because in the end, shouldn't beauty be fun?

covet:
tarte sun-kissed cheek stains
anne-claire petit accessories crocheted animals
patch jewelry
red flower moroccan rose body lotion
naturabisse honey body refiner
shu uemura take eyelashes
shu uemura deep sea water

eskell

designer-owned boutique

1509 north milwaukee avenue. between north and honore. blue line: damen
773.477.9390 www.eskell.com
tue - fri 11a - 7p sun noon - 6p

opened in 2005. owners: elizabeth del castillo and kelly whitesell
all major credit cards accepted
online shopping

wicker park >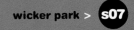

many, many years ago, vintage and new never dared to mingle in fashionable women's boutiques. let's say that they weren't friendly with each other. vintage meant moth-holed, frayed, past its prime. new meant shiny and clean and perfect. thanks to all of the sharp, modern retailers who think outside the box, we now can find superbly stylish vintage looks mixing like best friends with new looks. in their boutique *eskell*, kelly and elizabeth marry the two seamlessly, referencing both new and old to design their own fantastic line.

covet.
eskell dresses
covet tank with buttons
vintage cowboy boots
plastic island black & white dress
grace sun plum bubble-sleeve dress
in god we trust jewelry
silk bangle bracelets

foursided

a frame shop and gallery

5061 north clark street. between foster and lawrence. red line: argyle
773.506.8300 www.foursided.com
mon - fri noon - 7p sat 11a - 7p sun noon - 5p

opened in 2006. owners: todd mack and gino pinto
all major credit cards accepted
custom framing

andersonville > 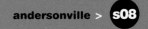 **s08**

it makes all the sense in the world that a fantastic framer would also be an artist. meet todd, artist, framer and co-owner of *foursided* which is part gallery, part frame shop. so you don't have any art to frame? you don't need art to enjoy this place as you can browse through vintage maps, photography and other antique objets. but if you do want something framed, they're able to make art out of ordinary objects by thinking outside the box—and inside of it—from memory boxes to floating frames. you'll soon learn that *foursided* is anything but square.

covet:
todd mack collages
vintage math flashcards
wrapping paper
vintage chicago maps
revamped old frames
vintage globes
plaster hands forms

113

gem

a jewelry shop

1710 north damen avenue. between wabansia and st. paul blue line : damen
773.384.7700 www.gemchicago.com
tue - fri 11a - 7p sat 11a - 6p sun noon - 5p

opened in 2005. owner: laura kitsos
all major credit cards accepted
online shopping. custom orders

bucktown >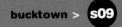

every summer growing up, it was a ritual to visit the annual local arts and crafts fair. this day was my absolute favorite because it meant perusing the stalls of local jewelry artists with my dad, and if i was really lucky, he would let me pick one piece from that season's sellers. *gem* is a miniature, urbane version of that fair for me. laura mixes her own beautifully handcrafted collection of jewelry with the work of other artful jewelers. if only dad were here to take me shopping.

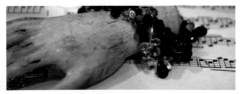

cover:
laura's designs:
  lucky cluster line
  vintage pendant necklaces
  black drusy pendant
bauxo reclaimed leather cuffs
kathy frey jewelry
rose cut diamond pendant
silver snake head necklace

greer

grand paper shop

1657 north wells street. corner of eugenie street. brown / purple lines : sedgwick
312.337.8000 www.greerchicago.com
tue - fri 11a - 6:30p sat 11a - 6p sun call for hours

opened in 2005. owner: chandra greer
all major credit cards accepted

old town >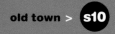

when i first met chandra, her stationery store was new, and the first *eat.shop chicago* was already on shelves. heartbroken that i'd have to wait two full years to spread the word in print, i have tried to tell everyone I know about *greer* for the last twenty-four months. well, here we are for the second edition, and i'm not out of gushing admiration yet. this gorgeous shop still astonishes and excites me every time I set foot in it. if everyone were to live her life as chandra lives hers, what a civilized and eloquent place the world would be.

covet:
chic office letterpress file folders
russell + hazel everything
millimeter/milligram books
good on paper sticky notes
little otsu annual weekly planner
paper + cup letterpress cards
handmade "psycho" dialogue books

grow

a modern children's boutique

1943 west division street. between damen and winchester. blue line : damen
773.489.0009 www.grow-kids.com
tue - wed, fri 11a - 6p thu 11a - 8p sat 10a - 6p sun noon - 5p

opened in 2006. owners: deree and kevin kobets
all major credit cards accepted
registries

wicker park >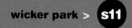

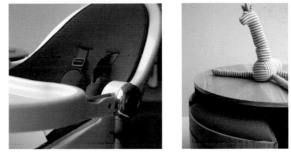

i hear that kids are smarter than ever these days, so it makes all the sense in the world to create a smarter kids' store, which is exactly what deree has done with *grow*. thoughtful, healthy, organic design for for all those smart new babies. if we're working on creating a better world for the next generation, shouldn't we start with their little worlds first? from disposable diapers to organic cotton onesies—at *grow*, you're stocking up while being kind to the planet, and the plus is you're getting some of the most mod looks around. green = good-lookin' at *grow*.

covet:
bloom baby high chair
orbit stroller
ige bird wood mobile
kate quinn organics clothing
dwell bedding
bloom baby rocker
oobe nest bassinet

habit

a design collective

1951 west division street. between damen and winchester. blue line : damen
773.342.0093 www.habitchicago.com
tue - sat 11a - 7p sun noon - 5p

opened in 2005. owner: lindsey boland
mc. visa

wicker park >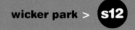

you know those before-they-were-stars features in magazines that make you wonder when someone from your own town is going to end up famous so you can say you knew her before she was somebody? well, if you want to get in on the pre-fame action, start shopping at *habit*, a designer collective for up-and-coming luminaries in the fashion world. lindsey manages to catch new talent as soon as they're out of the gates, filling her racks with local and indie fashion designers, including her own label, superficial. so come on over before i can say, i told you so.

covet:
superficial inc. shorts
i.sheff ruffled jacket
katrin schnabl dresses
nature vs. future jackets
abigail glaum-lathbury pants
tulina bags
tuyere belts

hejfina

lifestyle boutique for men, women and home
1529 north milwuakee avenue. between north and honore. blue line : damen
773.772.0002 www.hejfina.com
sun - mon noon - 6p tue - sat 11a - 7p

opened in 2004. owner: heiji choy black
all major credit cards accepted
online shopping. custom furniture

wicker park >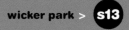

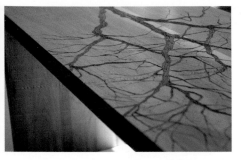

i can't help feel like i've stepped out of chicago and into an international city when i visit *hejfina*. heiji plays the role of curator here, reminding me of small european shops where you'll find a collection of things that may be varied in subject but coalesce together in style. things are generally more straight-forward here in the midwest, but heiji mixes that sensibility in with the more cosmopolitan. whether it's an international fave like martin margiela or local stars like michael koehler and f2 glass, the finds are always special at *hejfina*.

covet:
preen womenswear
loeffler randall flats
adam kimmel menswear
trosman necklaces
f2 glass
carson maddox furniture
michael koehler furniture
comme des garçons wallets

i.d. chicago

modern home and eyewear

3337 north halsted street. between buckingham and roscoe
red / brown / purple lines : belmont
773.755.4343 www.idchicago.com
tue - sat 11a - 7p sun noon - 5p

opened in 2001. owners: steven burgert and anthony almaguer
all major credit cards accepted
online shopping. registries

lakeview >

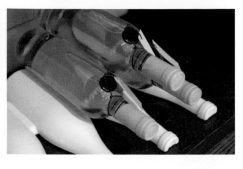

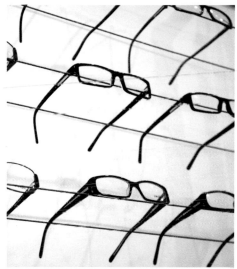

did you ever go through a phase when you didn't need glasses but you really wanted them? i did. i insisted to my mom that all of my russian lit reading was giving me headaches, which led to an eye exam, which led to the ever-so-slight need for a prescription, and i soon had a pair of tortoise-shell frames. i spent more time in front of the mirror than reading, but i was happy and headache-free. more than a decade later—and reading sans glasses—i find that desire tugging at me when i enter *i.d. chicago*, whose eyewear is just as appealing as its housewear.

covet:
transglass
prada sunglasses
blu dot rocker chair
harry allen hand hook
puddles by tord boontje
karim rashi stemware
improved crockery by esther derkx

125

josephine

elegant shoe salon

1405 north wells street. between schiller and north
red line : clark or division / brown line : sedgwick
312.274.0359 www.josephineonline.com
mon - sat 11a - 6p sun by appointment only

opened in 2003. owners: nicole rego shockley and danielle rego
all major credit cards accepted
online shopping

old town >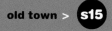

i couldn't let these shoes go: jil sander. hot pink. four-inch heels. slight platform. rounded toe. perfect for an end-of-summer wedding i was planning for. you'll most likely feel this i-must-have these-now feeling about the shoes at *josephine*, so it's all about pacing and control here. on second thought, forget that and go crazy. treat yourself to a shopping spree at the best spot in the city for finding candy for your feet. there is nowhere else around that has a selection like this, and with double help from twins danielle and nicole, you will walk home with very happy feet.

covet:
laurence dacade gold platforms
missoni pumps
rodo everything
blue patent rupert sanderson heels
martin margiela lucite heel wedge
etro flats
k. jaques sandals
jil sander bags

kara mann

designer showroom

119 west hubbard street, fifth floor. between clark and lasalle. red line : grand
312.893.7590 www.karamann.com
by appointment only

opened in 2007. owner: kara mann
ordering available through showroom

river north >

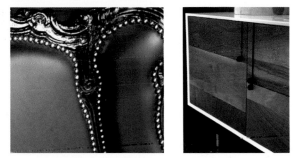

everyone has an idea of their dream home. it's half of the fun of making your home your own, even if you never reach the ideal—the fantasy is what motivates the creative process. when i took the elevator up to the airy penthouse where star interior designer kara mann has settled in, i realized my entire dream home was right there, within her showroom walls. with its majestic, punky elegance and dark decadence, this is the place for only the most serious of shoppers— or perhaps dreamers. you will find no peers for this world of style anywhere else in town.

covet:
jimmie martin custom scorpion chair
elson & company rugs
jean de merry leather chairs
ochre lighting
kevin cherry furniture
bddw furniture

komoda

eclectic gift store

2559 west chicago avenue. corner of rockwell. cta bus: 66 /65
773.276.8229 www.shopkomoda.com
mon - fri 11a - 7p sat 10a - 6p sun noon - 5p

opened in 2006. owners: sherri and dominik gregorczyk
all major credit cards accepted

west town >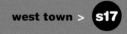

once in a blue moon, shopping loses its fun and it becomes a chore, something done out of necessity: grocery shopping, shopping for new socks or for the tenth wedding present for the season. the best detox regimen for this rut is a trip to *komoda*, where it's never a task to spend a fun afternoon browsing this general store of fun, finding trinkets and toys and cheer-you-up accessories and products. there will be some of what you need here, but a ton of what you'll want. just what the shopping doctor ordered.

covet:
pop ink soap
snow & graham gift paper
caswell-massey everything
livo different razor holder
folding fans
zodiac rose incense sticks
metal house numbers
l'aromarine fleurs blanches eau de toilette

koros

clothing store and art gallery

1019 west lake street. between carpenter and morgan. green / pink line : ashland
312.738.0155 www.korosartandstyle.com
sun - tue noon - 6p wed - sat 11a - 7p

opened in 2005. owner: kristen skordilis
all major credit cards accepted

west loop >  **s18**

when *eat.shop chicago* first came out two years ago, we celebrated with a party at *koros*. the food was delish, *eat.shop* business owners from across town came to mingle, but most of all, no one could stop shopping at this fantastic boutique. by the end of the night, kaie—fabulous founder of the *eat.shop guides*—and i were modeling cashmere sweaters for each other, debating over style and color. this is the sign of an excellent store, that even during a party, filled with good people, good food and good wine, you still can't keep away from the shopping.

covet:
hoss jackets
hoss black die-cut skirt
justice bodan belts
ted baker kelly green sandals
tori nichel dresses
strenesse white linen shirt
samantha goldberg jewelry

le magasin

french housewares

408 north clark street. between kinzie and hubbard
purple / brown lines : merchandise mart
312.396.0030 www.le-magsin.com
mon - sat 10a - 6p

opened in 2003. owner: didier milleriot
all major credit cards accepted
online shopping. registries

river north >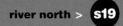

ah, the glory of the wedding gifts of yore! exquisite silver tea sets! fine table linens! elegant soup bowls! delicate china! today, registries are not quite so grand: suitcases. drills. food processors. today's focus is pragmatism, not posterity. i don't think i'll be saving my roller bag for generations to come, do you? *le magasin* manages to be practical and pretty at once, making it desirable to find long-lasting gifts that can still be used every day. i think even our great grand-mothers would have approved. no, not just approved; they would have loved didier and *le magasin*.

covet:
vintage hand towels
linens & tablecloths
plum glass goblets
aprons
bed linens
creamers
kitchen linens

135

merz apothecary

a classic apothecary

ls: 4716 north lincoln avenue. between leland and lawrence. 773.989.0900
macy's: 111 north state street. 312.781.4000
www.merzapothecary.com / www.smallflower.com (for online ordering)
north lincoln: mon - sat 9a - 6p macy's: mon - sat 9a - 8p sun 11a - 6p

opened in 1875. owners: abdul qaiyum, anthony qaiyum and michael winter
all major credit cards accepted

lincoln square / the loop > 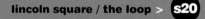 **s20**

one of my favorite things to do while traveling overseas is to explore the local drugstores. sometimes they're more apothecary, sometimes more beauty, sometimes more general store. but there is always some commonplace drugstore product (i.e. toothpaste) that seems cooler at these foreign spots. you can have this same experience here in chicago at *merz*, where this century-old place imports overseas drugstore favorites as well as the classics our parents and grandparents depended on. naturalist, homeopath, product-lover alike will all love *merz*.

covet:
dr. hauschka everything
nivea creme
claus porto bath soak
dresdnor herbal baths
radius toothbrushes
elgydium toothpaste
pre de provence soaps

nina

a well-knit shop

1655 west division street. between paulina and marshfield. blue line : division
773.486.8996 www.ninachicago.com
mon 11a - 7p wed - thu 11a - 7p fri - sat 11a - 6p sun noon - 5p

opened in 2004. owner: nina rubin
mc. visa
classes

wicker park > 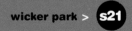 **s21**

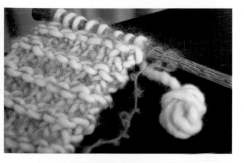

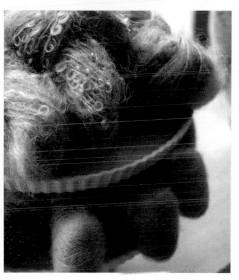

my other dream career—aside from this glorious one of eating and shopping my way through cities nationwide—is to own a knitting shop. mainly this would be so that i could spend every day knitting: crocheted bikinis in the summer, hats and mittens in the winter. since nina has already created the best knitting experience in town, it's hopeless to compete, so i'll gladly give in and shop here instead. local knitters keep nina, the owner, quite busy so she has little time for herself to get all her personal knitting projects done. nina, you deserve a little time off —to knit.

covet:
bulky hand-dyed alpaca
habu textiles mohair
classic cashsoft
bc sweet magic ball
blue sky knitting needles
blue sky organic cotton
suss yarns

139

ouest boutique

women's clothing with parisian style

1063 west madison street. between may and carpenter. cta bus: 20
312.421.2799 www.shopouest.com
mon noon - 6p tue - fri 11a - 7p sat 10a - 6p sun noon - 5p

opened in 2006. owners: kelly bry
all major credit cards accepted

west loop >

the most recent time i was in paris, i was only passing through, cruising from one train station to another and ogling the hoards of beautifully attired french women whom i was running by. i, a racing tourist, bag in hand, sweat beading, panic rising as the train's departure time neared, couldn't have looked or felt less chic. so *ouest* is my chance to redeem and clothe myself from head to toe in french-inspired fashion and to feel as fabulous as those parisians looked. i'll have to settle for strolling down michigan avenue instead of the champs élysée, but coming from *ouest*, i'll still be content.

covet:
sonia sonia rykiel red jacket
sport missoni dress
rozae nichols everything
dovelopment by erica davies jacket
barbara bui sweaters
paul & joe green and white shoes
jennifer ouilette headpands
habitual jeans

p.45

a women's boutique

1643 north damen avenue. between north and wabansia. blue line : damen
773.862.4523 www.p45.com
mon - sat 11a - 7p sun noon - 5p

opened in 1997. owners: tricia tunstall and judy yin
all major credit cards accepted
online shopping

bucktown >

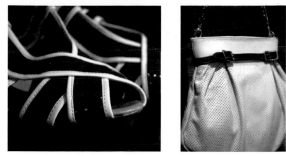

p.45 is like your longtime best friend, the one that had the "friends" half of the b.f.f. necklaces you wore when you were in grade school. that friend who, whether you see her every day or rarely, you fall right into sync with when you're together. which is exactly how *p.45* is. never has this store let me down. when i needed special gifts for my sisters or an all-white wardrobe for my all-white honeymoon (a shirtdress for traveling and a grecian summer gown), tricia and judy were the ultimate helpers and advice givers. pinky promise, they will always fall right into step with you.

covet:
patent leather dru flats
inhabit cardigan sweaters
mason everything
development blue & white striped dress
coven silver crocheted dress
lyell coats
toki jewelry collection

143

p.o.s.h.

antiques, treasures and traveler's finds

613 north state street. between ontario and ohio. red line : chicago
312.280.1602 www.poshchicago.com
mon - sat 10a - 7p sun 11a - 5p

opened in 1997. owner: karl sorensen
all major credit cards accepted
online shopping

river north >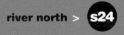

let's have a brief language lesson. the word posh—meaning smart, elegant and fashionable—has been around for almost a century. one theory is that the meaning came from the intials of port out, starboard home, which was stamped on tickets of first-class passengers traveling by sea between england and india in the mid-19th century. how aptly named is this store, nestled in the historic tree studios, culling together smart, elegant, flea-market finds and treasures from traveling. oh, the posh, posh traveling life, the traveling life for me!

covet:
argentine friendship rings
'50s vintage hand-tooled leather bag
chicago skyline plates
vintage hotel flatware
glass cake stands
vintage enamel numbers
'40s diner juice glasses

penelope's

1913 west division street. betwen winchester and wolcott. blue line : division
773.395.2351 www.penelopeschicago.com
mon - sat 11a - 7p sun noon - 6p

opened in 2002. owners: jena frey and joe lauer
all major credit cards accepted

ukranian village > 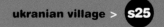 s25

we all know about peer pressure and how easy it is, at any age, to succumb to it. sometimes, sadly to say, we witness this pressure in boutiqueville, by seeing the same gosh-darn things at each place we step into. jena and joe must have been the truly cool kids in school, the ones who set trends, rather than followed them. looks like it did them well, as they're still setting trends at *penelope's*, which never yields to the phrase, "but everyone is doing it!" so give in to a little peer pressure from moi, and start shoppin' at *penelope's*.

cover:
wesc green & white stripe sweater
millimeter/milligram stationery
trovata purple dress
talla blouses
charlotte ronson wedges
a.p.c men's everything
sessun clothing
plastic island black & white skirt

porte rouge

home and table

1911 west division street. between winchester and wolcott. blue line : division
773.269.2800 www.porterouge.biz
mon - sat 11a - 7p sun 11a - 5p

opened in 2002. owners: kristin doll and grant drutchas
all major credit cards accepted
online shopping. registries

wicker park >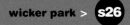

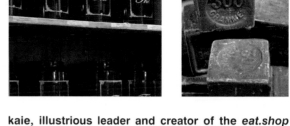

kaie, illustrious leader and creator of the *eat.shop guides*, is a serious tea drinker. i discovered this the first time i was at her house, and she casually offered me a cup of tea, leaving me to pick from the most comprehensive collection of options. i can't help think how kaie would love *porte rouge*, first and foremost a beautiful home store, and second, purveyor of mariage frères tea, sold in bulk in gorgeous tins. kaie, i think you're going to want to add a few more teas to your collection once you've made a trip to *porte rouge*.

covet:
green apple lamp berger
mariage frères tea
coucke kitchen linens
laguiole steak knives
savon de marseille french soaps
crystal decanters
dough-rising basket

primitive

furniture, jewelry and artifacts from across the world

130 north jefferson street. between randolph street and washington boulevard
green / pink line : clinton / lake
312.575.9600 www.beprimitive.com
mon - sat 10a - 6p

opened in 1988. owner: glen joffe
all major credit cards accepted

west loop >

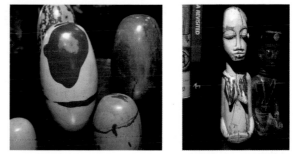

some objects have more meaning for us than others whether bestowed by us or gained through time. i travel with a special silver safety pin, whose presence comforts me. a treasured vintage map of the world seems to have hidden secrets. the necklace my grandmother wore as a child holds special significance for me when i wear it. *primitive* is full of objects that have meaning—protective amulets, powerful river stones and buddha statues. this is a haven for all who like a little meaning with their materialism.

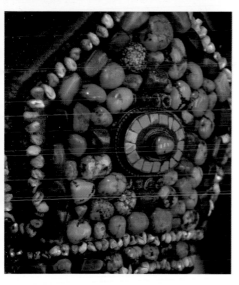

covet:
magic amulets
tantric lingams
oil lamp candelabra
ladakh crown
buddha room
mongolian saddle
elephant linguist staff
beautiful textiles

raizy

lingerie, bath and beauty shop

1944 north damen avenue. between armitage and homer. blue line : damen
773.227.2221 www.shopraizy.com
mon - sat 11a - 7p sun noon - 5p

opened in 2004. owner: renee gertzfeld
all major credit cards accepted
makeup application

bucktown >

i absolutely love the film *my fair lady*, where scrubby audrey hepburn gets fancied up and prettified and becomes the ultimate lady. who doesn't love a make-over story? i think of *raizy* as the place to spruce up in the beauty, bath and trousseau departments, and the place where the lov-er-ly renee will make you over, doing everything she can do help you smooth, tuck, tighten, brighten and beautify. her methods aren't quite so taxing as those of henry higgins, so you're certainly bound to have more fun than eliza doolittle ever did.

covet:
kobo candles
l'artisan perfumeur
leigh bantivoglio silk robes
cosabella
ren exfoliating body balm
velvet rope body lotion
jimmy jane massage oil

153

red dog house

a dog boutique

2031 north damen avenue. between armitage and dickens
blue line : western / milwaukee
773.227.7341 www.reddoghouse.com
tue - fri 11a - 7p sat 11a - 6p sun noon - 5p

opened in 2006. owners: steve and marice greenberg
all major credit cards accepted
online shopping. custom orders

bucktown >

i often get tempted to go out and get a new puppy to keep me company. i've picked the breed, and even her name. then i remember that i live smack-dab downtown—in a condo with no backyard, meaning early mornings in the middle of winter would be spent outside on the frozen sidewalk. i'm not so sure she's worth it. but then i go to *red dog house*, and all of that is forgotten. these folks ease the challenges of having an urban pooch, and make it downright irresistible with stylish toys and tasty pet snacks. maybe my little puppy will become a reality after all.

covet:
dog design name collar
chilly dog sweaters
pet revolution modern dog beds
happy tails travel dog collection
beggar's banquet madame fideaù treats
dog town bites
my doggy bones
fromm pet food

revival

architectural finds

1401 west irving park road. corner of southport avenue. red line : sheridan
773.248.1211 www.rerevival.com
daily noon - 6p

opened in 2003. owners: mark steinke and shemek drabio
all major credit cards accepted
online shopping

lakeview > s30

it seems the best things in life come with age. wine gains richness and complexity, novels turn into bookcase classics. antique silver develops a rich patina, relationships and friendships grow deeper with passing years. so it's no wonder that *revival* is a treasure-trove full of furniture and accessories that are growing more desirable and exceptional with time. mark and shemek pull together these vibrant pieces from the past—from antique wooden dominos to a polar bear cocktail shaker—that, in my eyes, need no reviving at all.

covet:
green simmons metal dressers
wood trough
snowshoe chairs
glass bell jars
polar bear cocktail shaker
tall black metal cabinet
lucite coffee tables
vintage glass lighters

robin richman

2108 north damen avenue. between webster and armitage. blue line : western
773.278.6150 www.robinrichman.com
tue - sat 11a - 6p sun noon - 5p

opened in 1997. owner: robin richman
all major credit cards accepted

bucktown >

berlin is one of my favorite cities. the stores are outstanding—tucked away, small little places with hand-sewn fashions. it's a city where you'll find anything but overly produced styles. each store carries items that seem to be one-of-a-kind, carefully created artistic visions. this is exactly how i feel about *robin richman*. this is largely because of robin herself, who has a vast collection of beautiful vintage trimmings that she uses to create belts, pins, and jewelry, and whose artistic hand touches every part of this store.

covet:
hannoh black & white striped dress
gary graham white dress
schiesser underwear
graham and spencer anything
johnny farah belts
goti jewelry
majestic paris t's

roslyn

a covetable women's clothing store

2035 north damen avenue. between armitage and dickens
blue line : western / milwaukee
773.489.1311 www.roslynboutique.com
tue - sat 11a - 7p sun noon - 6p

opened in 2006. owner: roslyn dulyapaibul
all major credit cards accepted

bucktown >

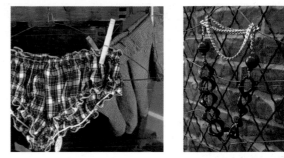

one of the features of this guide is a list of covetable items from each store. in most stores, i am drawn to a handful of things. from this short list, i cull my covets, and voila! my work is done. *roslyn* proved to be a major problem for me though, in a good way. i found myself coveting everything in the store, and my list grew far too long. rosie carries exactly what i want, and i'll bet you a pair of plaid steven allen undies it's what you'll want, too. as for me, i'm just copying and pasting my unedited covet list to this year's holiday wish list.

covet:
tony cohen white dress
bensoni tops
erica davies long dress
vera wang lavender label dresses
goldenbleu white clutch
sass & bide gold & black top
steven allen plaid underwear
long green nicholas k sweater

rotofugi

designer toy shop and gallery

1953 west chicago avenue. between winchester and damen. cta bus : 66 - chicago
312.491.9501 www.rotofugi.com
mon - sat noon - 8p sun noon - 5p

opened in 2004. owners: whitney and kirby kerr
all major credit cards accepted
online shopping

west town >  s33

since i spend my days looking for store owners who are doing something different than everyone else, i was very pleased the first time i came across *rotofugi*. whitney and kirby opened an unusual store in an off-the-beaten-path part of town (even more so three years ago), and have since developed a massive fan following of toy lovers and collectors. not only have they survived in their atypical niche, but they're growing—now with a gallery next door to the toy store. who ever said toys and art didn't go hand in hand? not i, not whitney, not kirby.

covet:
ciao ciao vinyl
mario - super mario dx3
circus punk diy blank
troglodyte - periwinkle
cabella plush
dudson's modern tales: heenie
shawnimal pocket fuzz
bearded prophets

saint alfred

a cool kicks shop

1531 north milwaukee avenue. between north and honore. blue line : damen
773.486.7159 www.stalfred.com
mon - sat noon - 8p sun noon - 6p

opened in 2005. owners: ian ginoza, eddy haus and david lin
all major credit cards accepted

wicker park >  **s34**

cool *eat.shop* sneaker stores unite! there's *bodega* in boston. *wthn* in philly. *status* in minneapolis. and here in chicago, *saint alfred*. whether you're a collector with a fervor on par with *entourage's* turtle character, or you had a stint of sneaker graffiti in high-school and doodled on your own converse hi-tops as i did, or you like the look of a little silver sneaks bling on your feets, this is the place for you. where amateurs and afficionados alike can appreciate the spread of street-cool footwear.

covet:
nikc airforce xxv
nike air max
air force 1's
vans
all star converse
reeboks
stussy
swagger from japan

scout

an urban antique shop
5221 north clark street. between foster and farragut. cta bus : 22 - clark
773.275.5700 www.scoutchicago.com
tue - wed 11a - 6p thu - fri noon - 7p sat 11a - 6p sun noon - 5p

opened in 2004. owner: larry vodak
all major credit cards accepted

andersonville >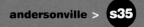

david o. selznick. jerry bruckheimer. harvey weinstein. larry vodak. all great producers, bringing together the finest talent to create a fantastic final product. wait, larry vodak—who's that? owner of the amazing *scout*, of course. larry has the best framer, the best lamp-reworker, the best furniture re-finisher. and of course, the best eye, which he uses to spy unusual finds to fill his shop. nothing sticks around here for long though, so my message to you is this: don't dally making a decision. that trophy piece you love will be on its way out of *scout's* door within days.

covet:
scott kruss photos
handcrafted iron mirror
stainless rolling cart
ted harris lamps
natural sponge baskets
steelwork table
botanical prints
wood cork lamp

soutache

embellishments and trimmings

2125 north damen ave. between webster and armitage. blue line : damen / western
773.292.9110
tue - sat 10a - 6p sun noon - 5p mon by appointment

opened in 2005. owner: maili powell
mc. visa
classes. custom orders / design

bucktown > 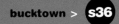 **s36**

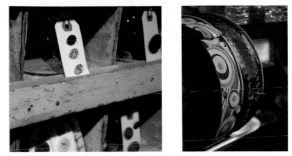

my mom has had forever an enormous wooden sewing cabinet. it's filled with every bit of frill and detail you could possibly add to a garment or handmade pillow—buttons, fancy snaps, rick-a-rack, ribbons. I used to think there didn't exist a more thorough source for all things fabric. but there does. *soutache* is like a mega-version of mom's crafty cabinet. here you can find every button, bag handle or ribbon that you might need to embellish or enhance. and just in case you weren't born with the crafty bone, then maili can custom-make just about anything you need.

covet:
round wooden bag handles
bamboo belt buckles
ribbons, ribbons, ribbons
buttons, buttons, buttons
knitting embroidery ribbon
workboard of ideas
feathers

sprout home

urban garden and home shop

745 north damen avenue. between chicago and superior. cta bus : 66 - chicago
312.226.5950 www.sprouthome.com
daily 9a - 8p

opened in 2003. owner: tara heibel
all major credit cards accepted
design & installation services. online shopping

west town >  **s37**

my dad has an aptitude for picking feeble fir christmas trees. one long-ago holiday, he revealed to me that our x-mas tree was so full of holes, he harvested the bushier areas for good branches, then drilled the trunk in several spots to fit the branches into the bare places. out of all of those beauties, he always chose one of the runts. so i adore *sprout home*, as my beautifully symmetrical, no-cosmetic-surgery-needed, christmas tree came from here last year. with all kinds of cool home stuff and everything you need to create an urban garden, this place is the ultimate indoor/outdoor shop.

covet:
rare ornamental trees
rooftop / deck container garden installation
organic co-op (monthly boxes of produce)
turquoise gourd bird apartment
garden-in-a-bag
sukie pillows
etra bench
mr. and mrs. jones juicer set

stitch

home, travel and accessories

1723 north damen avenue. between cortland and wabansia. blue line : damen
773.782.1570 www.stitchchicago.com
mon - fri noon - 7p sat 11a - 7p sun noon - 6p

opened in 1998. owner: pamela hewett
all major credit cards accepted
registries. online shopping. custom orders / design

bucktown >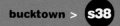

i have pieces from *stitch* throughout my house—the beautiful couch where i lounge every evening, the plates i eat from, the silverware i use every day. i have to confess that i married into such glorious home accessories (my husband was already an avid *stitch* shopper) that i couldn't be happier with the items, and i wouldn't have chosen any other supplier than *stitch*. you'll want to spoil yourself here—and don't let me stop you—but this place is especially good for spoiling others, when you're seeking out something special for a friend who needs a treat.

covet:
third drawer down limited-edition linens
not rational canvas camo diaper bag
nava design's one year of white pages
acme printed computer bags
innermost fantome ghost clock
hable constructiion pillows
kris nations resin bangles

the boring store

a spy store

1331 north milwaukee avenue. between paulina and wolcott. blue line: damen
773.772.8108 www.826chi.org
daily noon - 6p

opened in 2007
visa. mc

wicker park >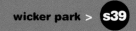

growing up the youngest of four, i've always had a bit of the spy bug in me. i tried to listen in on my sister's phone conversation with her prom date, and i devised ways to get insider info on siblings from overly chatty friends. *the boring store*, with its spy paraphernalia, would have helped me back then. a phone tap here, a decoy there. if only i'd had the proper arsenal. *the boring store* is a front to the spy store, and the spy store is yet another front for *826 chicago*, a non-profit student writing and tutoring center. want to know more? you're going to have to do a little detective work.

covet:
global positioning device
top-secret folders
pre-shredded documents
telescopes
waterproof surveillance notebooks
spybug
extra eyes
trench coat

the house of glunz

wine merchants

1206 north wells street. between division and goethe. red line : clark/division
312.642.3000 www.houseofglunz.com
mon - fri 10a - 8p sat 10a - 7p sun 2p - 5p

opened in 1888. owners: the glunz - donovan family
all major credit cards accepted

old town >

rule one: pasta should be eaten only at places where an italian works. rule two: the best hotdogs can only be found at places next to factories. rule three: men's clothes should only be sold by a woman (except a suit finely tailored by a man over fifty years old). these are just a few of the rules i've developed doing these books. *house of glunz* makes me consider a new rule: only buy wine that's in a dusty bottle—it may be the oldest wine store in chicago, with some beautifully aged wines, but it also sells recent vintages. this place gives character to even the most immature juices.

covet:
freemark abbey cabernet sauvignon bosche
04 dry creek heritage zinfandel
02 leoville poyferre, st. julian
domain meriwether, discovery cuvee sparkling
hirsch 16-year-old reserve bourbon whiskey
duchesse de bourgogne belgian ale
assorted cheeses & crackers

the sweden shop

gifts from scandinavia

3304 west foster avenue. corner of spaulding. brown line: kimball
773.478.0327 www.theswedenshop.com
mon - sat 10a - 6p sun 10a - 3p

opened in 1950. owner: patty rasmussen
mc. visa
registries

northwest side >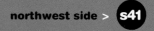

when my mom lived in chicago in the seventies, *the sweden shop* had already been around for twenty years. she would go there to pick up wooden clogs and traditional swedish accessories and gifts. now, more than thirty years later, this gem is still going strong after a recent makeover. if you have a love affair with lotta jansdotter like i do, this is the place where you can find her designs and the best of other scandinavian design from marimekko prints to anne black ceramics. for cloggers, don't worry—you'll still find a comfy clog selection in the back room.

covet:
lotta jansdotter everything
anne black ceramics
karin eriksson ceramic coffee cups
marimekko aprons
sukie sticky notes
filippa k. for rorstrand
kosta boda mine! glassware
tord boontje midsummer light

twosided

cards, antiques and gifts

2958 north clark street. corner of wellington. brown / purple lines : wellington
773.244.6431 www.foursided.com
mon - fri noon - 7p sat 11a - 7p sun noon - 5p

opened in 2003. owners: todd mack and gino pinto
all major credit cards accepted

lincoln park > 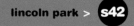 **s42**

in a box in my desk, i store cards for most every occasion: birthdays, weddings, engagements, new babies, father's day, mother's day—anything you can think of that elicits celebrating—i've got a letterpress paper product for it. in order to keep this box well supplied in all of its many categories, i'm on the prowl everywhere i go for contenders. so when i recently came across *twosided*, sibling store to the frame shop *foursided*, i was thrilled to find such an extraordinary supply. looks like i can go straight to the source from now on.

covet:
cards by:
  yellow bird greetings
  smudge ink
  hammerpress
  egg press
  coffee stain
  driscoll design
great gift items

white chicago

new, sample, and once-wed designer wedding gowns

222 west huron street. between franklin and wells
brown / purple lines : chicago
312.397.1571 www.whitechicago.com
tue - wed 11a - 7p thu 11a - 8p fri 11a - 6p sat 10a - 6p

opened in 2006. owners: ursula guyer and stacy senechalle
mc. visa
alterations

river north >

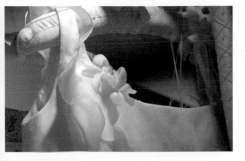

even before i came here with my sister-in-law-to-be, i was enamored with *white chicago*, a place to feel like a bride without feeling too bridey. with its pristine head-to-toe white interiors, it's possibly the most striking boutique in the city. enticed by *white chicago's* word of mouth, bridget came here on her gown search. lo and behold, she experienced the quintessential wedding gown story—love at first sight with first dress she tried. that fall she married my brother, in her ivory satin and lace, and ursula and stacy had yet another blissful bride story to tell.

covet:
wedding dresses:
 badgley mischka
 lazaro
 reem acra
 monique lhuillier
 vera wang
 yumi katsura

willow

cool stuff from indie designers

908 north damen avenue. between walton and iowa. blue line : division
773.772.0140 www.shopwillow.net
tue 11a - 7p wed - fri 11a - 7p sat 1 - 6p sun noon - 4p

opened in 2005. owner: amy doehla
visa. mc

ukranian village > 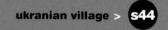 **s44**

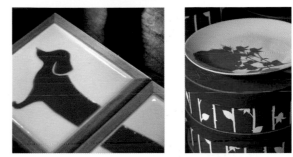

having recently spent a little time touring brooklyn's collection of interesting shops—designer co-ops and collectives brimming with super cool, covetable objects—*willow* seems more than ever like a direct import from the new york borough. you'll find this store full of stuff that you won't find anywhere else in town. where else have you seen a monkey ashtray with a moveable mouth in chicago? amy has done her homework and knows what chicago doesn't have but could really use; she knows where the edge is, and how far to push it.

covet:
lonfisk tea set
smp message beans
green & associates plates and cups
pangea organics lavender hand soap
modern twist coasters
skull villa ashtrays
sarah cihat china

wolfbait & b-girls

local designers boutique

3131 west logan boulevard. at milwaukee. blue line: logan square
312.698.8685 www.wolfbaitchicago.com
tue - thu noon - 7p fri - sat 10a - 7p sun 10a - 4p

opened in 2006. owners: shirley novak and jenny stadler
mc. visa
classes. fashion styling

logan square >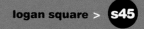

have you ever taken a pair of scissors to a piece of your clothing? a pair of jeans turned to shorts? a rough-hewn sleeve on a t-shirt during a deconstruction phase? it's always fun to do minor clothing re-design remembering those distant lessons from home-ec. if you ever get that itch again, come to *wolfbait and b-girls*. not only are owners jenny and shirley inspiring to watch working in their shop/studio, but they also give classes for those of us who want to create also. and if your work is worthy, maybe you'll be one of the local designers selling at their shop.

covet:
nice lena earrings
vika jackets
brazen judy clothing
bruiser clothing
light from the moon bangles
haley handmades sachets
mohop shoes

wright

boutique and auction house
1440 west hubbard street. between armour and noble. green/pink line: ashland
312.563.0020 www.wright20.com
by appointment / open to the public for auctions

opened in 2000. owner: richard wright
all major credit cards accepted

west loop >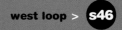

wright is a virtual art history lesson in modern design. perhaps if my college art professors had used the shopping angle with me, all of those names and eras might have really stuck. class field trips could have been made to the spacious *wright* warehouse of goods, where we could have experienced what it is like to sit on chairs created by gio ponti. just like paying a visit to the art institute's architecture and design collection but better. and at *wright*, if you really love it, you can take it home with you.

covet:
harry bertoia sculpture
santiago calatrava stools
zaha hadid woosh sofa
pierre jeanneret conference chair
george nakashima slab coffee table
gio ponti lounge chairs
maison jansen chairs
franco albini tables

notes

notes

etc.

the eat.shop guides were created by kaie wellman and are published by cabazon books

eat.shop chicago second edition was written, researched and photographed by anna h. blessing

editing: kaie wellman   copy editing: lynn king   fact checking: emily withrow
additional production: julia dickey

anna thx: all of the amazing businesses featured in this book. kaie, for creating such gosh-darn swell books. katie, for her countless recommendations. shawn, for his ideas, words, opinions and company.

cabazon books: eat.shop chicago second edition
ISBN-13 978-0-9789588-8-6

the eat.shop guides are distributed by independent publishers group: www.ipgbook.com

to find more about the eat.shop guides: www.eatshopguides.com

PRINTED IN SINGAPORE